THE LEGAL SIDE OF BUYING A HOUSE

a Consumer Publication

edited by Edith Rudinger

published by Consumers' Association
publishers of **Which?**

Consumer publications
are available from
Consumers' Association
and from booksellers.

ISBN 0 85202 231 9
and 0 340 38254 6

Photoset by Paston Press, Norwich
Printed and bound in Great Britain by
Hazell Watson & Viney Limited,
Member of the BPCC Group,
Aylesbury, Bucks

THE LEGAL SIDE OF BUYING A HOUSE

a Consumer Publication

Consumers' Association
publishers of **Which?**
14 Buckingham Street
London WC2N 6DS

CONTENTS

INTRODUCTION

Buying a house is probably the biggest single purchase most people ever make. It often proves an emotional as well as a material investment. But the actual legal process of buying a new home can be slow, complicated and costly. And even the stout-hearted among us may find it a harrowing experience.

The house transfer system in England and Wales is fragmented, involving solicitors, estate agents, surveyors, building societies, banks, local authorities and so on. Almost inevitably, given the number of people involved, delays occur while one has to wait for the other. In addition, until not all that long ago, it was generally believed that it was illegal or impossible for a layman to do his own conveyancing – that is, buy or sell his house – without employing a solicitor. That is not true, but until quite recently only solicitors were allowed to charge for conveyancing, and competition was therefore limited. The mould was broken with the publication of the first edition of *The legal side of buying a house* back in the sixties, which demonstrated that it was possible to do your own conveyancing, and so save money and maybe save time.

The system of house transfer is now changing. Consumers' Association has spearheaded the campaign and, spurred on by a CA-drafted private member's bill in 1983, the government has introduced legislation to make the business of conveyancing in England and Wales more competitive. This legislation has ended the solicitors' virtual monopoly on conveyancing, and paved the way for non-solicitor conveyancers. A council for licensed conveyancers is being set up to draw up the detailed rules needed to protect the consumer against incompetence, negligence and fraud on the part of the new professionals, and to issue licences to those who satisfy the requirements that are laid down. (If you go to an unlicensed non-solicitor conveyancer, there is no guarantee that he will meet the professional requirements laid down by the council.)

Although it may be some time before we see these licensed conveyancers in competition with solicitors, the legislation is proving just the right fillip to reduce costs, stimulate innovation and speed things up.

First, solicitors' conveyancing charges are coming down. Until recently, you could expect to be charged two per cent of the purchase price of a property for the buying side of the conveyancing. Today, you would be more likely to pay only one per cent or even one-half per cent for the same service. Charges vary greatly, though, even within the same town, so for anyone who chooses to go to a solicitor it is well worth shopping around.

Second, the legal profession is meeting the challenge of competition with a welter of new ideas. For example, some solicitors are able to sell property in England and Wales following the example of their scottish counterparts. Some individual firms of solicitors have even opened their own estate agents' offices, charging a combined fee for conveyancing and estate agency. A national association to promote solicitors' property centres was formed in 1984, with a growing membership within the legal profession, which indicates that many solicitors want to widen their interests into estate agency.

The first solicitors' property centres opened last year (1985) in Crawley and Wrexham, but others could soon be springing up all over the country. The new centres were formed by groups of local firms of solicitors, and are run by managers who have experience in buying and selling property, employed by the solicitors. Their combined estate agency and conveyancing fee may work out cheaper than the fees charged separately by solicitors and estate agents.

With solicitors widening their interests in house transfer, it is hardly surprising that others involved in the system want to do the same. For example, estate agents argue that they should be allowed to do conveyancing as well. And building societies and banks may be able to offer conveyancing services of some sort in the future.

In the new climate of reform, other changes are taking place. An important one concerns the checking of 'title' – that is who, in fact, owns a property. Information about title in some areas is registered with the Land Registry. This is being expanded to cover parts of the country where registration is not yet compulsory, and it is being computerised. A computerised service should make the checking out process a lot quicker.

Consumers' Association has also campaigned to open the register to the public. Access to the register is at present restricted to the owner of the property and anyone authorised by the owner (and certain public bodies such as the police). An open register would enable people readily to find out who is the owner of a house or piece of land. And it could well speed things up, because a conveyancer would not need authorisation first before inspecting the register.

Sellers – or their conveyancers – are starting to play a greater role in speeding up house transfer. For example, some sellers' solicitors apply for local authority searches when a house first goes on the market and make them available to buyers.

Sellers could do more, though. Indeed, it is likely that the government's permanent conveyancing committee, set up to find ways of further streamlining and simplifying house transfer, and above all, of breaking house-buying/selling chains, will look closely at how sellers could become more involved.

As important as these developments is the change of attitude by professionals and public bodies involved in the house transfer system (which is what Consumers' Association has long campaigned for). Many of them – solicitors, estate agents, building societies and so on – now recognise the importance of working more closely together to effect a simpler, quicker, less costly system. They recognise that consumer choice in conveyancing services is now a fact of life. *The legal side of buying a house* is also about choice – it demonstrates that do-it-yourself conveyancing is a viable alternative to conveyancing by solicitors or other professionals.

without a solicitor

With all these changes in house transfer taking place, is it still worth doing your own conveyancing? There are several reasons why you should at least consider it:

- Despite reduced conveyancing charges by solicitors, you can still save hundreds of pounds by d-i-y conveyancing, even though there are some costs you cannot avoid such as local search fees and land registration fees and possibly stamp duty.
- A big advantage of d-i-y conveyancing is that you are largely in control of events. It does away with the frustration of chasing up your solicitor to get him to chase up the seller's solicitor. You can dictate the pace and possibly eliminate delays.
- With a few exceptions, d-i-y conveyancing is straightforward. Provided the house is a secondhand one, at present occupied by an owner-occupier and the title to it is registered with title absolute, there is no reason why you should not be able to buy (or sell) it without employing a solicitor.

with a solicitor

It would be wrong to ignore the reasons for using a solicitor or other conveyancer. The savings made by d-i-y conveyancing may not be great if you need a mortgage. For example, although a bank or building society will not insist that you should use a solicitor for your side of the conveyancing, it will insist that the mortgage side is done by a solicitor – for which you are charged. Usually, if you decide to use a solicitor, he will do the building society work as well, and charge an all-in fee. If you do your own conveyancing, you will be charged more for the building society work.

D-i-y conveyancing means that you are on your own, more or less. If you make a mistake, it could cost you more than a few sleepless nights, whereas solicitors have professional indemnity insurance so that any such mistakes or problems should be resolved at no cost to you.

Using a solicitor may prove more successful or indeed essential in certain circumstances, due to the time-honoured practice of 'undertakings' between such professionals. The seller's solicitor, or the bank manager, may accept an undertaking from the buyer's solicitor, possibly even in the form of a few words over the telephone, where he would not or could not accept such an undertaking from a layman.

It would not be wise to do your own conveyancing if the person you are buying from (or selling to) is doing his own conveyancing as well and neither of you have mortgages. In these circumstances, there would be no solicitor in the background, primarily employed to do the mortgage side of the conveyancing, who would be aware of problems or any major errors.

And if you are selling your present house and buying one in a different part of England or Wales, the distances may make it impracticable to do your own conveyancing which involves personal attendance at certain stages of the process.

follow Matthew Seaton

Whether or not you choose to do your own conveyancing, this book provides an invaluable account of the conveyancing process. It describes in detail the procedure to be followed where a person is buying a house with registered title for his own occupation from an owner-occupier. To this end we will follow an imaginary buyer, Matthew Seaton, who will guide us step by step through the buying of a house, 14 Twintree Avenue, Minford. We shall then describe the transaction from the seller's point of view. If nothing else, this book exposes the myth that it is impossible for the layman to do his own conveyancing.

CONVEYANCING

Why should buying or selling a house be more complicated than buying a watch, a car, yacht or freezer? Land, which in legal terms includes any buildings on it and everything over and under it, has always been the tangible basis of our social, economic and political life, and the uses to which land can be put are legion. The law reflecting this is therefore also complex.

Land is permanent, lawyers call it 'real'. It can be handed down from generation to generation, from father to son, aunt to nephew. Two or more people can own the same piece of land at the same time, husband and wife, business partners and any others. Many and various third party rights can exist in land and can be enforced against its owner, such as rights of way, mineral rights, sporting rights and restrictions as to its use. Land invariably adjoins other land, so mutual rights and obligations arise between neighbours, such as rights of support. The nature and enforceability of these rights and obligations may differ according to how the land is built on, for example houses or flats. Lastly, because the availability of land in our country is limited it is subject to strict governmental control through planning legislation, health and safety regulations, conservation measures and many others.

To get an inkling of what is involved in buying and selling a house, imagine seeing a new freezer on sale in a store. On reading the sale particulars you discover that the store cannot define its exact boundaries, that Mrs Brown has a right to put one block of ice-cream in the second freezing compartment every thursday, that you must not use it for storing frozen peas, and that you need planning permission to place a toaster on top of it.

A solicitor or licensed conveyancer has to be fully conversant with these complexities and, if you employ him, he takes over the responsibility of buying or selling your house. Whether you are buying or selling (or both), he has to ensure that your transaction is absolutely foolproof. If you are buying, he deals with such matters as thoroughly investigating the seller's title to the house and asking appropriate enquiries of official or other bodies; if selling, he answers enquiries on your behalf, proves your title to the house, and obtains due payment of the purchase price.

registered and unregistered land

In England and Wales all land is either unregistered or registered, and there are two quite distinct methods of transferring (or conveying) the ownership of each. Under the unregistered system, every time the property changes hands, the buyer must make a fresh investigation of the title offered to him, to satisfy himself as to the validity of the seller's title, that is, his right to sell the property. He has to investigate the documents of title (known as title deeds) covering at least the past fifteen years, to make sure that the property was correctly transferred to previous owners. Proving or investigating title to unregistered land can be extremely lengthy and technical. If you are contemplating buying or selling a house with unregistered title, you should employ a solicitor or licensed conveyancer.

Towards the end of the last century, an alternative method of conveyancing was introduced into this country, the registered land system; in its modern form it dates from the Land Registration Act 1925. This system is administered by a government department called the Land Registry, in accordance with the terms of the Land Registration Acts 1925–1971 and various rules made under them. Put simply, the idea behind the system is to substitute a title guaranteed by the state (in the sense that compensation is payable for mistakes and omissions made by the Land Registry) for the separate investigation of title. Title to a property is investigated once only by the Chief Land Registrar or, more accurately, his staff, when he receives an application for first registration. An authoritative record of the title is prepared (the register) describing the land with the rights it enjoys, naming the current owner and detailing most of the burdens to which the land is subject. Thereafter this record is kept current by a regular updating of the information kept in it. The register is the registered owner's proof of title and he receives an official copy of it, called a land certificate, as evidence of his title. (If the property is subject to a mortgage, the lender is issued with a charge certificate and the land certificate is retained by the Land Registry.)

In theory, the result is that a prospective buyer of registered land need not concern himself with the history of his seller's title. By a simple examination of the register, he can verify that the seller has the power to sell the property and can discover the exact nature of any rights over it, or interests in it. It has been said that the register is 'a mirror which reflects accurately and completely and beyond all argument the current facts that are material to a man's title'. Undoubtedly this greatly simplifies the buying and selling procedure but the words 'in theory' should sound a note of warning right at the outset. The register is not a complete record of all matters affecting registered property. It was intended to replace the separate investigation of title, but it was not intended to relieve a buyer of his task of personally inspecting the property he intends to buy. Therefore certain rights and interests in registered land, with the common characteristic of being usually easily discoverable on careful inspection, remain valid and will bind a buyer despite their not being mentioned on the register. They are called 'overriding interests' and will be described more fully later on in the book.

Whether or not a property is subject to the registration of title depends, with the exception of council houses, on whether it falls within an area of compulsory registration.

The system of land registration has been introduced gradually. Now approximately eighty-five per cent of the population of England and Wales live in areas of compulsory registration. The compulsory areas include all the large urban parts of the country such as London, Manchester and West Yorkshire. Even in these areas, registration of a previously unregistered property is only compulsory when it is next sold, although the owner of unregistered property can apply for registration at any time.

Outside the compulsory registration areas, registration is not possible, except in a limited number of cases specified by the Chief Land Registrar and where special statutory provisions apply. It has always been government policy to extend the registered system to the whole of England and Wales. Until recently, progress has been sluggish and spasmodic. But as part of the present shake-up of house transfers, the government has undertaken to speed up and extend the programme of introducing compulsory registration, which they hope to complete by 1994.

is it registered?

You can find out whether a particular place is in a compulsory registration area by asking the Land Registry (Lincoln's Inn Fields, London WC2A 3PH, telephone 01-405 3488) for explanatory leaflet No. 9, which they will send you free of charge. The leaflet sets out the districts in England and Wales in which registration of title is compulsory and gives the district land registry for each county. A supplement to leaflet No. 9 (also free, but you have to request it especially) shows the date on which a particular area becomes a compulsory registration area. The longer a particular area has had compulsory registration of title, the more likely it is that a particular property there is registered. Eastbourne was made a compulsory area in 1926 and most property there is now registered, having been sold at least once since 1926. However, Arun, not many miles away, was only designated a compulsory area in 1978, so relatively fewer properties there have registered title.

You can tell whether your title is registered if you have a large folder entitled 'Land Certificate' with your deeds. If you have bought your property with the aid of a mortgage, the document will be entitled 'Charge Certificate', but will be in the possession of your building society or other lender.

Do not attempt to use this book if the property you are buying does not have a registered title. It describes only the procedure to be followed where an owner-occupier is selling a house with registered title absolute to a person who wants the house for his own occupation.

There are some other situations when you should use a solicitor or licensed conveyancer.

if a newly-built house In the case of a newly-built house, the buyer's solicitor or licensed conveyancer must ensure that the contract provides for the house itself to be properly built. He must see that the boundaries are correctly shown on the plans, that the seller will construct new roads, drains and so on as are appropriate, that his client (the buyer) is granted any necessary rights of way, drainage rights and similar rights, and that any restrictions imposed by the seller are fair. Once these matters are settled for the first buyer they are fixed more or less unalterably for the future, so that a subsequent buyer (or his solicitor or licensed conveyancer) is in the position of having to take things as they stand. On a subsequent sale or purchase, the solicitor has to explain any shortcomings to his client, but the legal work involved in a second or subsequent purchase is much less than on the vital first purchase.

if parts are let Complications can arise, primarily under the Rent Act legislation, where part of the property is let and the buyer is taking over a sitting tenant. In such a case it is advisable to get legal assistance. The rights of a residential tenant are fully explained in the Consumer Publication *Renting and letting*.

if buying a council house The Housing Act 1980, as amended, lays down the procedure for local authority tenants to buy their council house. Such a purchase is not dealt with in this book but is described in the Consumer Publication *Renting and letting*.

for some leases The procedure described in this book is inappropriate, too, for cases where a person takes a lease at a rent (not a ground rent) without paying a capital sum for the lease. (This, too, is dealt with in *Renting and letting*.)

This does not mean that leasehold property is excluded from consideration here. It is quite common, especially in London, to find a house where an owner-occupier is the holder of a lease which he has bought for a capital sum – that is, the property is leasehold not freehold. Legal difficulties do arise at the time when the lease is first granted, usually when the house is first built, and such cases are outside the scope of this book. Once the lease is granted, however, the procedure is much the same as on the sale of a freehold, assuming the title to the lease is registered. It will be registered if the title to the land was registered when the lease was granted and the lease was for a term of more than 21 years. It will also be registered if the lease was of unregistered land within a compulsory registration area and was granted for a term of not less than 40 years. If it was of unregistered land not then (but later) within a compulsory registration, it will be registered if it was sold with more than 40 years left of the terms to run after the area was designated one of compulsory registration of title.

The terms of the lease may be a little more difficult to understand and the process of buying and selling more lengthy, because some extra investigations may be necessary.

flats and maisonettes The buying and selling of a flat or maisonette is also outside the ambit of this book. Although the title to a flat or maisonette may be registered, problems can arise over the enforcement of mutual rights and obligations, the use and maintenance of common parts, insurance, and repairs of the main structure.

business premises Finally, buying or selling business premises are excluded from this book; totally different considerations apply to them.

you can do it yourself

So – provided that the house (which includes terrace or semi-detached houses, cottages and bungalows) is a secondhand one, at present fully occupied by an owner-occupier and the title to it is registered with title absolute, there is no reason why an ordinary person should not be able to buy and sell it without employing a professional conveyancer.

but beware Having decided to do your own conveyancing, either on buying or selling a house, it is important to realise that it may prove impossible for you to succeed in carrying it through. In guiding the imaginary Matthew Seaton through his purchase and sale we mention many of the pitfalls, legal or otherwise, that may befall you. If one or other of these problems makes it impossible for you to continue with your own conveyancing, you should immediately consult a solicitor or licensed conveyancer. He may charge you the same fee he would have charged had he handled the transaction right from the beginning and may be scathing about your efforts so far. But you should not let this deter you from going to him, if you are in any real doubt or difficulty.

The chart on pages 194 to 196 shows the approximate time it takes to buy or sell a house with registered title and outlines the conveyancing procedure in four stages:

stage one : preliminary
stage two : contract to completion
stage three : completion
stage four : after completion

BUYING

The main participants

THE BUYER

Matthew J Seaton
138 Broadstone Drive
Hastings, Sussex

THE SELLER

William H and Margaret E Timms
14 Twintree Avenue
Minford, Surrey

THE SELLER'S SOLICITORS

Dodds & Son
1 Charter Street
Minford, Surrey

THE BUYER'S BUILDING SOCIETY

Forthright Building Society
88 Lomax Street
Minford, Surrey

THE SELLER'S BUILDING SOCIETY

Minford Building Society
102 Great Winchester Street
Minford, Surrey

THE BUYER'S BUILDING SOCIETY'S SOLICITORS

Hodgson, Green & Co
67 Lomax Street
Minford, Surrey

THE SELLER'S BUILDING SOCIETY'S SOLICITORS

Anderson, James & Pringle
88 Great Winchester Street
Minford, Surrey

THE BUYER'S INSURANCE COMPANY

Bridstow Insurance Co Ltd
403 High Street
Guildford, Surrey

THE SELLER'S ESTATE AGENTS

Flint & Morgan
43 High Street
Minford, Surrey

THE BUYER'S AND BUILDING SOCIETY'S SURVEYORS

Andrew Robertson & Co
22 Hamilton Street
Minford, Surrey

STAGE I – PRELIMINARY

Matthew Seaton, a young accountant and his wife Emma, a veterinary student, have been saving hard to buy a house of their own since they got married four years ago. Just after Christmas, Matthew learnt to his great surprise that a relative of his who had died had left him a legacy of £15,000. This, added to their savings, meant that they now had about £18,000. Matthew had spoken with the manager of the Forthright Building Society (with whom they were saving) and learnt that, taking into account his current earnings, he should have no difficulty in obtaining a mortgage for £30,000, provided that the property they decided to buy was considered satisfactory. In most cases, if building societies are satisfied about the applicant's financial status, they would provisionally agree the amount of loan with the applicant, subject to valuation of the property when it is found. (One society may give a 'mortgage certificate' which confirms how much the applicant can borrow.)

the estate agent

When Matthew and Emma received particulars of 14 Twintree Avenue, Minford, Surrey, from Flint & Morgan, one of the firms of estate agents they were dealing with, they went to see the house immediately and fell in love with it. Mr and Mrs Timms the sellers wanted £46,000 for the house and although they refused to accept anything lower, they did agree to include all the curtains and fitted carpets at present in the house in this price. They had hoped to sell these separately. £45,000 was the limit Matthew and Emma had set themselves, but they liked the house so much and were happy with the arrangement over the curtains and carpets.

The next day, Matthew went into Flint & Morgan's offices and told Mr Morgan that he wished to buy 14 Twintree Avenue. Mr Morgan was expecting him, he had already spoken on the telephone with his clients. He knew what had been arranged about the curtains and carpets.

It is useful to ask the estate agent at this stage

- whether the title to the house is registered
- whether anyone other than the seller and his family is living in the house (for example, a tenant) and
- the name of the local authority.

Mr Morgan did not know whether the title was registered but assumed that it was, since Surrey had been a compulsory registration area since 1952 and he thought that the Timms had only lived in the house for about ten years. He told Matthew that the local authority was Minford District Council and confirmed that no one other than Mr and Mrs Timms was living in the house.

It used to be the practice to leave a small deposit, say £100, with the estate agent, to show that you are a serious buyer. This is no longer the normal procedure, so if you are asked for a preliminary deposit, check that you are dealing with a reputable firm of estate agents before you actually hand over any money. If you pay such a deposit in cash, you should obtain a receipt on the spot. It is as well to make clear that payment of such a deposit is 'subject to contract and survey', just in case something goes wrong later and that it is held by the agents as stakeholders.

Mr Morgan then enquired which solicitor would be acting for him in his purchase, to which Matthew replied that he would be doing his own conveyancing. Mr Morgan said he would pass this information on to Mr and Mrs Timms' solicitors who would start the ball rolling.

mortgage application

Most people need additional finance to buy a house and Matthew was no exception. You do not need a solicitor's help to apply for a mortgage, although he may be able to advise you on where to go for a loan if the particular circumstances of your case – such as your age, income or occupation – make it difficult for you to obtain finance in the ordinary way, or to advise on the type of mortgage. The estate agent who is selling the house can be helpful in finding a lender, too. He may have an extra incentive to help, if he gets a commission from the body providing the finance when a mortgage is successfully negotiated. And he will get his commission from the seller on the sale of the house which the mortgage has made possible.

Matthew would get his loan from the Forthright Building Society where he and Emma had their savings invested. The other main source of finance for buying a house is a bank. All things being equal, a potential borrower doing his own conveyancing would be granted a home loan (even though some banks would prefer the conveyancing to be done by someone qualified). The bank would require a qualified solicitor to act for it, to supervise the transaction, and the costs of this would have to be borne by the borrower, as they would if the lender is a building society.

The Consumers' Association book *Which? way to buy, sell and move house* includes a chapter on mortgages, explaining the difference between a repayment and an endowment mortgage and how building societies assess a potential borrower's income and how they decide what his borrowing limit should be. It gives details of the costs connected with obtaining a mortgage and has a brief note about MIRAS, that is tax relief on the interest payable on up to £30,000 of a mortgage loan.

From whatever source a mortgage loan is sought, it will take some time to make the arrangements. Forms must be filled in, the lenders will check references about the buyer's financial position and prospects. They will also want to have the property inspected to make sure that it is one on which they are willing to advance the amount of the loan.

Matthew went straight from the estate agents to see the manager of the Forthright Building Society, told him that he hoped to buy 14 Twintree Avenue and that he would like to apply for a loan from the society of £32,000, approximately 70 per cent of the purchase price. The manager gave him an application form which asked for information about himself and the house. He was also given a form requiring him to list all the persons who would be living in the house and to inform the society of any change in this list before the loan was made.

An applicant can take the forms away to fill them in at home, but most building societies prefer that the application papers are completed in the branch office. This gives the building society the opportunity to discuss the application fully and to raise the question of life insurance and buildings and contents insurance, and so on.

Where the applicant is a d-i-y conveyancer, the building society should give details of its panel solicitor and the charges the borrower will have to pay for the work done by the lender's solicitor (and also the surveyor/valuer). If these details are not given automatically, ask for the information.

amount and type of mortgage

When the manager fills out an application form with the would-be borrowers, he takes into account the main income, together with any regular bonus, overtime or commission. In general terms, a building society would consider lending approximately two and a half to three times the main income plus the second income, in determining the maximum size of the mortgage. However, this is where the interview helps the manager, not only to consider the present situation, but also to assess the longer term prospects. In establishing a size of loan which a couple may manage, he takes into account their ability to meet outgoings not only at the start of the mortgage, but also for the foreseeable future.

In addition to satisfying himself that Matthew and Emma could afford the mortgage of £32,000, the manager also explained the difference between the two main types of mortgage – repayment and endowment.

With a repayment mortgage, each month's payment is composed partly of interest and partly of capital. Thus at the end of each year, when they receive their statement of account, Matthew and Emma will see a reduction in the initial balance of £32,000. During the life of the mortgage, interest will be charged on this reducing balance. Therefore, with less of each month's payment needed for interest, more will be available for capital repayment, until the mortgage is cleared at the end of the mortgage term – in their case, 25 years.

By contrast, an endowment mortgage involves a separate transaction with a life insurance company. Matthew and Emma could insure themselves singly or jointly for the amount of the mortgage advance. They would pay premiums to the insurance company direct, relating to the value of cover required. In this way, for the premiums paid, the insurance company would provide, in 25 years' time, sufficient money to clear the mortgage, plus – in most cases, depending on the type of policy – profits in excess of the mortgage cover, which would then be for Matthew and Emma's use. Were either Matthew or Emma to die during the 25 year life of the mortgage, the insurance company would clear the mortgage by paying £32,000 to the Forthright Building Society.

If Matthew and Emma decided on an endowment policy of this sort, it would be assigned – the ownership legally handed over – to the building society. The manager then explained that once this had been done, the repayment of the £32,000 capital was assured: it would be repaid in 25 years' time or earlier on the death of either Matthew or Emma. Therefore, since the building society knew it would get its money back in due course, it would agree to accept monthly payments of only the interest necessary, and maintain the balance in being at the £32,000 borrowed. Thus with an endowment mortgage, there is no need for the additional part payments of capital on a monthly basis, which apply in a repayment mortgage.

If Matthew and Emma chose an endowment mortgage, therefore, their monthly payments would be lower than for a repayment mortgage, since these would contain only interest with no element of capital. However, it would be necessary to add the cost of the monthly premiums to the insurance company to the interest-only mortgage payments to the building society.

The manager reminded them that they could expect to get tax relief from the Inland Revenue based on the interest paid each year – but not on any repayment of capital. If they decided on an endowment policy, the tax relief would be on an unchanged basis – because no repayment of capital was due for 25 years. If, on the other hand, they chose a repayment mortgage, the amount of interest (and therefore the tax relief applicable) would reduce as the capital outstanding gradually reduced over the 25 year period.

The manager made the point that under present legislation, tax relief was in any case only available up to £30,000. Therefore, on the first £30,000, interest would be charged at the full rate less tax relief at 30%, while the full rate would then be payable on anything above £30,000.

The manager realised that Matthew and Emma would need a day or so to discuss the best type of mortgage for them, find out more about the various types of endowment policies and, if applicable, to obtain quotations from several life insurance companies. He therefore agreed to leave the application open for this final decision and pointed out that the application could then proceed immediately they had made their decision. (If they decided on a repayment mortgage, nothing more was needed; even if they decided on an endowment mortgage, the application could proceed once they had agreed a policy with a reputable life insurance company and given the details to the building society. The handing over – assignment – of the policy could take place later.)

valuation and survey

The manager then explained that once Matthew had completed the application form, he would instruct the society's valuer to make arrangements to inspect the house and prepare a valuation report. All building societies and most other lenders require such a report before lending money on the mortgage of a house. The property is the security for their money; if a buyer defaults on repayments, they must make sure that the proceeds of sale of the property would be sufficient to repay the loan and all arrears outstanding.

The buyer has to pay the surveyor's valuation fee which, though no longer on a fixed scale, is generally based on the purchase price of the house (not the amount of the loan). Matthew learnt that he would have to pay a valuation fee of £69 (including

VAT). It is important to realise that a survey made on behalf of building societies or other lenders is for the purpose of valuation, to advise them how much to lend and on what terms. It is not necessarily adequate for a buyer, who would be well advised to obtain an independent structural survey. Neither building societies nor sellers guarantee that a house is structurally perfect (or even fit for human habitation), although you would probably have some come-back against the building society's valuer if the house actually collapses.

A certain duty of care exists in the relationship between the building society's valuer and the borrower for whom the valuation has been carried out, but an offer of advance may expressly exclude any warranty as to the state of the property. If in the course of his inspection the building society's valuer sees items of disrepair or major structural problems, he would report this to the building society. However, the surveyor is acting for the building society (or other lender) when he prepares a valuation report, not the buyer of the house.

If the building society's valuation report is made available to you, remember that all the society or lender is interested in is the value of the property. Under our law, a buyer is subject to the rule of *caveat emptor* (buyer beware), even when it comes to buying a house. A buyer takes property subject to any defects which he could have discovered by inspection by an expert eye whether or not an expert inspection has taken place. That is why it is advisable to have an independent structural survey carried out, by a reputable surveyor.

Matthew asked the manager of the Forthright Building Society to let him know which firm of surveyors would be preparing the valuation report, so that he could instruct them to do an independent survey of the house for his own benefit.

It is quite normal to employ the same surveyors as are preparing the valuation for the building society. You will probably save money on fees by doing this, as there need be only one visit by one professional surveyor to the house. Some building societies will not tell borrowers the name and address of the valuer who will be carrying out the inspection. Or if the surveyor is on the staff of the building society he may not be able to carry out a private structural survey at the same time. On the other hand, some building societies offer their mortgage applicants the choice of three different types of report and valuation:

a basic report and valuation which is a copy of the valuation and report prepared for the society for the purpose of determining whether or not the property forms a suitable mortgage security

a more comprehensive report and valuation in one of the forms offered by the Royal Institution of Chartered Surveyors or the Incorporated Society of Valuers and Auctioneers; or

a full structural survey the fees for which are by negotiation and are additional to the building society's normal scale fee for the basic report and valuation.

The cost of an independent survey should be agreed in advance. It depends on the size of the house and the time spent there and how thorough a survey is required. If the house is still furnished at the time when the surveyor is to make his examination, he will not be able to make as detailed a survey as if the house were empty. The surveyor may advise against buying the house unless he is given the chance to make a thorough examination.

It is not only for old property that it is desirable to have a survey done: a recently-built house can have serious defects too, through bad design, bad workmanship or neglect.

the correspondence starts

On the friday, Matthew received his copy of the memorandum of sale from Mr Morgan accompanied by a covering letter and a copy of the estate agent's sale particulars of 14 Twintree Avenue.

FLINT & MORGAN
Surveyors Estate Agents

43 High Street
Minford, Surrey

9 January 1986

MEMORANDUM OF SALE, SUBJECT TO CONTRACT

Property sold:	14 Twintree Avenue, Minford, Surrey
Vendor:	Mr William H Timms & Mrs Margaret E Timms 14 Twintree Avenue, Minford, Surrey
Purchaser:	Mr Matthew J Seaton 38 Broadstone Drive, Hastings, Sussex
Purchase price:	£46,000
Fixtures and fittings:	purchase price to include fitted carpets and curtains
Particulars/plan:	attached
Other conditions:	none
Completion date:	to be agreed
Local Authority:	Minford District Council
Other information: (if applicable)	(a) mortgage required: yes/~~no~~ (b) mortgage source: Forthright Building Society, 88 Lomax Street, Minford, Surrey (c) purchaser's property: ~~sold/unsold~~ inapplicable
Vendor's solicitor:	Dodds & Son, 1 Charter Street, Minford, Surrey
Purchaser's solicitor:	Purchaser acting for himself

Signed by
Flint & Morgan

Copies of this memorandum sent to the vendor, the purchaser, and the vendors' solicitors.

Matthew put the memorandum, covering letter and sale particulars on his file. It is advisable to keep a file of all correspondence, documents and so on regarding your purchase. They will also come in useful later on any re-sale of the house.

the forms you will need

It is a good idea to obtain the forms you will need for your house purchase well in advance, from Oyez Stationery, a subsidiary of The Solicitors' Law Stationery Society. There are Oyez shops in Birmingham, Bradford, Bristol, Cardiff, Leeds, Liverpool, London, Manchester, Norwich (later in 1986) and Sheffield, where the forms can be bought. Or you can order by post from Oyez House, Third Avenue, Denbigh West Industrial Estate, Bletchley, Milton Keynes, MK1 1TG (telephone 0345 515171):

2 prints of Enquiries before contract **(Conveyancing 29 [Long])**

2 prints of Supplementary enquiries before contract **(Con 29 [Supplementary])** (for a first time buyer)

2 prints of Enquiries of district councils (**Con 29A** for district councils in England and Wales) *or* **Con 29D** Enquiries of local authority (for London)

1 print of Register of local land charges, Requisition for search and official certificate of search **(LLC1]**

2 prints of Requisitions on Title **(Conveyancing 28B)**

4 prints of Transfer of Whole **(Form 19** or, for property being bought by joint buyers, **Form 19[JP])**

1 print of Application by Purchaser for Official Search with priority in respect of the whole of the land in the title **(Form 94A)**

1 print of Application for an official search (bankruptcy only) **(Form K16)**

1 print of Application to register dealings with the whole of titles **(Form A4)**

1 print of Application for Office Copies **(Form A44)**

Matthew decided to order an extra print of all the forms, just to be on the safe side in case he made some mistake in filling in the forms. He telephoned Oyez House to find out the cost of these forms including postage, packing, VAT and handling charge. He then wrote off for them enclosing a cheque made out to Oyez Stationery. Instead of phoning first, it is of course possible to send an 'open' cheque, with an upper limit of, say, £10.50.

All except the enquiries and requisitions forms can also be bought from Her Majesty's Stationery Office.

If you go in person to buy the forms, ask the sales assistant to make sure they are the most up to date prints, not leftover older editions.

One other form a buyer needs is a land valuation form **Stamps L(A)451** which can be obtained from Inland Revenue stamp office (you will find the address in the telephone directory).

the draft contract

A week later Matthew heard from Dodds & Son, Mr and Mrs Timms' solicitors.

DODDS & SON
Solicitors

1 Charter Street
Minford, Surrey

To: M J Seaton Esq

16 January 1986

Dear Sir,

Re: 14 Twintree Avenue, Minford

We understand that you propose to purchase the above property from our clients Mr and Mrs W. H. Timms at the price of £46,000 (to include fitted carpets and curtains), subject to contract. We further understand that you propose to act without a solicitor on your purchase and have informed our clients of this.

We enclose draft contract in duplicate for your approval, together with office copies of the entries on the Register and filed plan.

Yours faithfully,

Dodds & Son

Under the council of the Law Society's rules of conduct, a solicitor should point out to his client (in this case, the seller) that he is dealing with an unrepresented person and that this could lead to complications and delay, even where this is quite unlikely to be the case. It may persuade the seller to seek a sale elsewhere.

Dodds & Son had enclosed a draft contract. Most solicitors in England and Wales use a printed form of contract, either the Law Society's Contract for Sale (currently the 1984 revision) or the National Contract for Sale (currently the 20th edition). These printed forms, when completed, contain the necessary basic terms of a contract; the names of the parties (seller and buyer), the property and the price. They also lay down standard conditions which regulate the rights and duties of the seller and the buyer and special conditions relating to the particular transaction in hand. The seller's solicitor decides which of the two forms of contract to use. Both contracts enjoy equal popularity and can be bought by members of the public from law stationers.

The draft contract Matthew received incorporated the Law Society's general conditions of sale (1984 revision). It was on a bright pink piece of paper folded down the middle to form four pages. On the front page were the basic details of the agreement he had made with the Timms, on the inside pages twenty-five general conditions and on the back page seven special conditions. A draft contract is the basis for negotiation between the parties and this is why Dodds & Son had sent the draft in duplicate. When its final form had been agreed, Matthew would send back to them one of the contracts amended as appropriate.

the Law Society's Contract for Sale (1984 Revision)

The front page of the contract was headed THE LAW SOCIETY'S CONTRACT FOR SALE (1984 REVISION) and was divided into a series of panels in which the basic details of the transaction had been filled in. The top panel began 'Agreement made . . .' with a space for inserting the date of the contract. Dodds & Son had pencilled "Do not date" in the space. The date would be written in on exchange of contracts. After the word BETWEEN was typed the full names and address of Mr and Mrs Timms, as 'Vendors', and

Matthew's full name and address, the 'Purchaser'. Then followed a brief summary of the transaction: 'It is agreed that the Vendors shall sell and the Purchaser shall purchase in accordance with the following special conditions the property described in the particulars below at the price of *forty-six thousand pounds (£46,000).*'

The second panel contained this description of the property: 'PARTICULARS – ALL THAT freehold/~~leasehold~~ property known as 14 Twintree Avenue, Minford, Surrey'. If the house had been a leasehold one, there would have been included here a reference to the lease: its date, who granted it originally and to whom, the period covered by the lease and the ground rent. Directly underneath the particulars was a printed instruction to "see back page" of the form for the special conditions of sale.

the deposit

Then came a thin panel, on the left-hand side of which *£46,000* has been typed against 'Purchase money', and *£4,600* against 'less deposit paid' leaving a 'Balance' of *£41,400* to be paid on completion. Condition 9 of the general conditions provides that a buyer shall pay the 'normal deposit' to the seller's solicitor on or before the date of the contract or such lesser sum as the seller shall have agreed in writing. 'Normal deposit' is defined in condition 1(f) as ten per cent of the purchase price. The 10% includes any preliminary deposit that may have been paid to the estate agents as soon as a sale is agreed. Flint & Morgan had not asked Matthew to pay a preliminary deposit. Nowadays estate agents usually only require a preliminary deposit in respect of a new house on an estate and then they call it a 'reservation fee'.

Condition 9 recognises that some buyers cannot afford to pay a full 10% deposit. This commonly happens where the buyer is selling his existing house for less than he is paying for his new house. The deposit he gets from his buyer (even if the full 10%) will not be enough to pay a 10% deposit to the seller. Asking the seller to agree to a reduced deposit saves him having to seek and, usually, pay for finance elsewhere. The seller may, however, be unwilling to accept a reduced deposit if he needs the full 10% to pay the deposit on his new house. If the seller does agree to take a reduced deposit and later has to serve a 'notice to complete' on the buyer, because of the latter's delay, the buyer has then to pay the 10% deposit in full. This is to ensure that the seller is adequately compensated should the sale fall through, through no fault of his own.

The draft contract for 14 Twintree Avenue stated that Matthew would have to pay a 10% deposit when the contract was made. He was quite happy with this arrangement as he had ample funds in the building society.

Whether you pay a 10% or lesser deposit, condition 9 says it must be paid by a solicitor's cheque or banker's draft. Obviously, you will have to use the second alternative. A banker's draft is a cheque signed by a bank manager (or one of his staff) so there can be no doubt that it will be met on presentation. What differentiates a banker's draft from a normal cheque is not the signature but the status of the body on which it is drawn. A banker's draft is a promise to pay from a bank with all the financial resources behind it and thus is unlikely to be returned unpaid.

So that exchange of contracts will not be delayed unnecessarily, you should inform your bank that you will be needing a draft for the deposit. You can go to any branch of your bank (take identification with you); your own bank will be notified and you can collect the banker's draft from any branch you specify.

Finally, condition 9 states that the deposit shall be held by the seller's solicitor as a stakeholder. This means that he may not give the deposit (or any part of it) to the seller without the buyer's permission. A special condition (added on the back of the form) may require that the deposit should be paid to the solicitor as 'agent for the vendor', which means that the solicitor does not have to retain it until completion and would have to pass it on to the seller if the seller asked him to do so. If the seller needs your deposit to pay the deposit on his new house, his solicitor will ask for the deposit to be held by him as 'agent for the vendor'. It is difficult for you to object to a request of this nature if you are part of a buying and selling chain and have in turn asked the same of the buyer of your house. But it does mean that you cannot be assured of regaining your deposit should your purchase fall through, through no fault on your part.

price of fittings

Against 'Chattels, fittings etc' on the front page would be written the figure, if one had been agreed, which the buyer was paying for items on the property which the seller had not included in the purchase price, such as light fittings, furniture or perhaps even a garden shed. Sometimes it is useful and indeed quite normal practice to agree and state separately the total value of items the seller is leaving behind, in order to reduce the purchase price and consequently the stamp duty payable when the house is eventually transferred.

Stamp duty is payable to the government on certain documents, including deeds transferring houses. At present, no stamp duty is payable on the transfer of a house where the price is not more than £30,000. Where the buying price is £30,001 and over the rate of stamp duty is one per cent of the purchase price. So bringing the price down below the threshold by separating out the price of fittings is particularly relevant where the price of the house is just over £30,000. However, stamp duty can only be saved in this way if the price for the chattels bears a reasonable approximation to their true value. And the buyer must inform and get the approval of the building society or bank which is lending the money.

Matthew made a note to ask Dodds & Son if £1,000 could be attributed to the curtains and fitted carpets. The purchase price of the house would then be £45,000 and Matthew would save £10 in stamp duty.

To the right of the purchase price, deposit etc. was a box for signing the contract when the time came, which was likely to be in about two or three weeks. In the bottom space on the front page, the name and address of Dodds & Son was typed against 'Vendor's solicitors' and that of Minford District Council and Surrey County Council against 'Local Authorities'. The space for the name of the 'Purchaser's solicitors' was, of course, left blank. Matthew was doing his own conveyancing.

the special conditions

Matthew now turned the contract form over. The back was headed SPECIAL CONDITIONS. Clause A said that the property was sold subject to the general conditions printed on the inside, in so far as they were not varied by or inconsistent with the special conditions on the back of the form, but that general condition 8(5) shall apply in any event. General condition 8(5) applies to the transfer of a leasehold house only. When the property is transferred, the seller impliedly promises, amongst other things, that all the terms of the lease have been complied with. Condition 8(5) modifies this promise regarding the state and condition of the property: the seller does not promise that the repairing obligations under the lease have been fulfilled, and this fact must be recorded in the deed of transfer. The words 'in any event' ensure that this modification occurs even where the seller sells as 'beneficial owner' (which is another word for absolute owner): they do not mean that the parties cannot alter 8(5) by special condition if they wish.

Special condition B expanded on some of the terms in the general conditions.

contract rate

Dodds & Son had inserted "5% above the base rate from time to time of Barclays Bank" as the 'contract rate'. If no contractual rate of interest is agreed between the parties and specified here, the fall-back rate of interest under general condition 1(b) will be the rate payable by an acquiring authority when taking over property under compulsory powers. This is laid down intermittently by the Treasury, by statutory instrument: *the Acquisition of Land (Rate of Interest after Entry) Regulations*, and whenever it is changed, the new rate is published in the *Solicitors' Journal* (available from law stationers).

The contract rate is important to both buyer and seller, for two reasons. First (under general condition 22), where there is a delay in completion the party in default (if any) has to pay the other compensation for late completion. The party entitled to compensation can choose to take interest at the contract rate on the balance of the purchase price for the period of default instead of suing for ordinary damages. And second (under general condition 18), the contract rate governs the amount of interest payable by the buyer on the balance of the purchase price if he is allowed to go into occupation of the property before completion.

completion date, specified bank, latest time

Next Matthew read that "contractual completion date is 7th March 1986." This was the date he and the Timms had agreed upon only last week. But they could have waited to fix a date when matters were more advanced, nearer exchange of contracts. If no completion date is specified when the contract is made, general condition 21(1) states that it shall be the twenty-fifth working day after the date of the contract.

Nothing was written next to the words "the specified bank is .....". The purchase money is usually paid by banker's draft and general condition 21(2)(b) limits the range of banks whose drafts are acceptable on completion to CHAPS (which stands for clearing house automated payments system) settlement banks. They are: Bank of England, Bank of Scotland, Barclays Bank plc, Central Trustee Savings Bank Ltd, Clydesdale Bank plc, Co-operative Bank plc, Coutts & Co, Lloyds Bank plc, Midland Bank plc, National Girobank, National Westminster Bank plc, Royal Bank of Scotland plc, Williams & Glyn's Bank plc. But the condition does allow a buyer to include within the range an otherwise unauthorised bank, by inserting its name in special condition B – provided, of course, the seller agrees. This was unnecessary in Matthew's case. His bank was Lloyds, a CHAPS member.

Against "the latest time is" was typed "2.0 p.m." This meant that Matthew had to pay the money due on completion date (friday 7 March) by 2.0 p.m., otherwise, by virtue of general conditions 21(5)(a) and (b), completion would be deemed to take place on the next working day (monday 10 March) and he might have to pay the Timms compensation for his delay of three days. (Compensation is calculated by reference to all days, not just working days.) Had no time been filled in, 'the latest time' would have been 2.30 p.m. The whole idea of specifying a time as well as a date for completion is to facilitate the banking arrangements of the parties, especially for a chain of buyers and sellers.

working days
General condition 1(g) defines working day as any day from monday to friday inclusive except Christmas Day, Good Friday, any statutory bank holiday and any other day specified in special condition B. Neither the sellers nor Matthew wished to make any other day a non-working day, so that the words "the following are not working days" could be crossed out.

Matthew noted that under the general conditions, the periods governing the procedural steps a buyer and a seller have to make from contract to completion were all calculated by reference to working days.

retained land
The words "the retained land is" had been crossed out. They would only have been relevant had the Timms been selling part of their land to Matthew and retaining some other part. In this case, general condition 5(3)(b) would have allowed them to keep (in legal terms 'reserve') certain rights, such as a right of way or right of drainage, over 14 Twintree Avenue for the benefit of their 'retained land', which (under general condition 5(3)(a)) would have to be adjoining 14 Twintree Avenue or land nearby and described in clause B.

special condition C: *opportunity to rescind*
Clause C referred to general condition 4 which only applies if expressly incorporated by clause C. General condition 4 gives the buyer a limited right to back out of the contract (lawyers say 'rescind') and recover his deposit if certain matters come to light after the contract is made which the buyer (or his solicitor) did not know about when contracting. Should this happen, the buyer must inform the seller or his solicitor in writing of his intention to rescind and his reason for so doing, within 20 working days from the date of the contract, unless clause C sets a different time limit. The matters justifying rescission are: if the property is subject to a financial charge (for example a road charge) which the seller cannot or will not pay off; if there is some law which prevents the buyer from continuing to use the property for the purpose which the seller has been using it, or for some other purpose stated in clause C; or if it turns out that there

is something likely to reduce the open market value of the property. This last ground is extremely wide and covers, for example, matters brought to light by the survey.

Most sellers' solicitors will exclude general condition 4 from the contract, because it means that, although the buyer knows that the property cannot be sold to someone else unless he decides to rescind, the seller cannot be sure that he has a sale until 20 working days have elapsed after the contract was made. But the seller may be forced to accept the inclusion of general condition 4 if, for example, he wants the buyer to exchange contracts in a hurry without being given time to have a survey and to make his usual enquiries and inspections. Then he or his solicitor will normally try to shorten the period during which the buyer has the opportunity to rescind (by using the words in brackets in clause C ". . . the period shall be *14 working days*").

Dodds & Son had specified that: "General condition 4 shall not apply." This was fine so far as Matthew was concerned. He was not going to exchange contracts until he had completed all his pre-contractual tasks.

special condition D: *types of ownership*

In clause D, "The Vendor shall convey as . . ." the seller has to state the capacity in which he is selling the property. His capacity dictates the number of promises (called implied covenants for title) the law presumes him to give to the buyer in the deed which eventually transfers the property. Theoretically the importance of these promises to the buyer is that once he becomes the owner of the property, his rights under the contract come to an end, so that if anything goes wrong his only remedy is to sue the seller for damages for breach of his implied covenants for title. And the more covenants there are, the better off he is. In registered conveyancing, a seller's title is state-guaranteed so, provided that the nature of the title being sold is 'absolute' (which most titles are), the capacity in which the seller sells and the covenants for title he gives are of little or no importance.

This said, the best capacity a seller can convey in is as 'beneficial owner'. This imports the widest possible implied covenants for title and means that the entire estate (that is, ownership) in the property is vested in him. Mr and Mrs Timms could have conveyed as 'beneficial owners' because between them they completely owned 14 Twintree Avenue. They were, however, selling as 'trustees'. Wherever land is concurrently (that is, at the same time) owned by two or more people, be it husband and wife or any other persons, the law says that they hold the legal title to the land on trust for themselves as beneficiaries. Technically speaking, the terms of the trust are to sell the land and distribute the proceeds. 'Trustees' only give one covenant for title. Since it is the seller's privilege to draft the contract, Mr and Mrs Timms could choose to sell as trustees, because thus they need only give one covenant instead of many. Nevertheless Matthew was amply protected if he ensured that the two trustee co-owners were parties to the deed of transfer and both signed it. If you come across a husband and wife selling as 'trustees' you probably cannot compel them to sell as 'beneficial owners'.

A trust to sell land and distribute the proceeds can also be used by someone who, either during his lifetime or on his death, wishes to benefit members of his family in succession, say his son and then his son's children. Here the legal title to the land will be vested in trustees (not necessarily the son or his children) and when they sell they too will only give one covenant for title – they convey as 'trustees'. But, again, the buyer is safe provided at least two trustees are parties to the deed.

Very rarely you may come across a tenant for life. He too sells as 'trustee' because he is only entitled to enjoyment of the property (called settled land) for his lifetime or some other limited period. After his death, or the happening of some other event, it passes to others in accordance with the terms of an existing will or trust (called a settlement). Again all that the buyer need do is check that the person he is dealing with is the registered owner and that at least two trustees of the settlement are parties to the transfer.

Where registered land is subject to a trust for sale or a settlement, there will be a restriction on the register to the effect that any proceeds of sale from the property must be given to at least two trustees, and naming them.

special condition E: *types of title*
Clause E told Matthew what class of title the Timms had, the title number and the district land registry. It read: *'The Vendor's title is registered with absolute title under Title No. SY43271604 in the Tunbridge Wells District Land Registry'.* General condition 12 provides that once contracts have been exchanged, and to prove his title, the seller of registered land must supply the buyer with the documents specified in section 110 of the Land Registration Act 1925. These documents include an authority to inspect the register, office copies of the entries on the register, the filed plan and any documents noted on the register in so far as they are relevant to the property. An office copy is an authenticated copy of an official document issued by the department or organisation which holds the original. The seller must also supply copies of documents creating, or evidencing any rights affecting the property, as to which the register is inconclusive or which are not required to be registered – for instance, where the seller has granted a lease of the property for less than 21 years.

An authority to inspect the register is necessary to make an official search of the register. The procedure for this is described later in the book. Where a solicitor makes the search on the buyer's behalf, he has to certify that he has the seller's permission to inspect the register and so, to save time, the authority is incorporated into the contract by clause E.

The words: "The Vendor authorises the Purchaser's solicitors to inspect the register and to obtain office copies thereof", were, however, inappropriate in Matthew's case. Since he was acting for himself on his purchase he would, later on, have to send the Timms' written authority for him to inspect the register with his application for an official search to Tunbridge Wells district land registry. This authority would be sent to him after the contract was made, together with an authority to inspect the register for the solicitors of his mortgagees, the Forthright Building Society.

The office copies and other documents mentioned in section 110 of the Land Registration Act are usually sent to the buyer with the draft contract. Matthew noted the pile of office copies Dodds & Son had sent him. He would study them in detail after he had finished reading the contract.

The alternative clause E applies to unregistered land only.

special condition F: *vacant possession*
Clause F then went on to say that the property was being sold with vacant possession. This meant that the house would be totally empty when Matthew completed the purchase and no tenants, or lodgers, or any refuse such as discarded furniture, would be there when Matthew came to move in. If the house had been subject to an existing tenancy, full details of it would have been given here in the alternative clause F. If there is any entry against the alternative clause F in a draft contract sent to you, you should not proceed but seek the help of a solicitor. Matthew thought that if there was undue delay, he might want or need to go into occupation before completion, provided Mr and Mrs Timms agreed. He did not have to suggest that anything be added to clause F to cover this. General condition 18 specifically sets out the rights of the buyer and seller should this happen.

special condition G: *stipulations*
Finally clause G read as follows: "The property is sold subject to the restrictions and stipulations referred to in Entry number 1 on the Charges Register of the above mentioned title number SY43271604, so far as they are subsisting and capable of being enforced or of taking effect. A copy of the said restrictions and stipulations having been supplied to the purchaser he shall be deemed to purchase with full knowledge thereof and shall raise no requisition or enquiry with regard thereto." Matthew looked at the office copies Dodds & Son had sent him and saw that a number of restrictive covenants were indeed set out in the charges register. He would look more closely at these later.

Having got to the end of the draft contract, Matthew realised that no provision had been made for the fitted carpets and curtains. If the Timms were happy to sell them to him separately for £1,000 and reduce the purchase price of the property to £45,000, there would need to be a special condition to this effect. If, on the other hand, the Timms insisted on leaving the purchase price of the property at £46,000, the special condition would have to state that the fitted carpets and curtains at present on the property were included in the purchase price.

the National Contract of Sale (20th edition)

Your seller's solicitor may equally well have sent you a draft contract form incorporating the National Conditions of Sale, which is on a pale blue piece of paper (instead of the Law Society's bright pink). The paper is folded down the middle to form four pages and the National's standard conditions are laid out on the inside two pages, in the same way as the Law Society's general conditions. The National's standard conditions cover much the same areas as the Law Society's general ones do, but there are fewer of them (22 as opposed to 25) and they are numbered differently. In some instances their content differs, especially where time limits are concerned. Most of the important differences are either mentioned here or as Matthew's purchase proceeds. There are, in fact, two forms of National Contract, one with special conditions and one without, but it is the former (with special conditions) that you are most likely to come across.

The first page is headed: 'CONTRACT OF SALE. The National Conditions of Sale, Twentieth Edition'. It is divided into panels, with a different layout from that of the Law Society's Contract and deals with the agreed rate of interest and the completion date on page 1 of the contract rather than by special condition.

The top panel will contain the full name and address of the seller ('Vendor'), and the buyer ('Purchaser').

The second panel is divided into two. On the left-hand side in the top box, headed "Registered Land", the district land registry and title number of the property will be given. Underneath this, in a separate box, the 'Agreed rate of interest' will be shown – probably 4 to 5 per cent above the base rate of one of the major clearing banks. If no rate of interest is inserted here, the 'prescribed rate' of interest under the National conditions is the same as the fall-back 'contract rate' under the Law Society's general conditions, namely the rate payable by an acquiring authority under compulsory powers. Under National condition 7, it is only the buyer who may have to pay interest at the prescribed rate on the balance of the purchase money if there is a delay in completion. (Law Society general condition 22 envisages payment of interest for late completion by "the party in default", the buyer or seller.) The 'prescribed rate' will also govern the amount of interest a buyer has to pay (under National condition 8) if he goes into occupation of the property pending completion.

The right-hand box of the second panel will contain details of the purchase price, deposit and price of items to be sold separately (if any). National condition 2 provides that the buyer shall pay a deposit of 10 per cent of the purchase price to the seller's solicitor on the date the contract is made. The National conditions make no express provision for the payment of a lesser deposit. If the seller is willing to accept one, this will have to be dealt with by special condition.

Then comes a large panel in which, under the heading "Property and interest therein sold" a description of the property will be filled in. In Matthew's case it would be: "Freehold property known as 14 Twintree Avenue, Minford, Surrey".

Underneath the description is a thin panel for the seller to state the capacity in which he is selling the property, next to the words "Vendor sells as". (In the Law Society's contract, the seller is required to state the capacity in which he sells in special condition D.) Further along the same panel is a space for inserting the completion date. If no date is agreed, National condition 5 states that completion shall take place 26 working days after the date of the contract or delivery of the seller's proof of title (that is, when the buyer receives it), whichever is the later.

The bottom panel of the contract contains a brief summary of the whole document: "AGREED that the Vendor sells and the Purchaser buys, etc. . . ." There then follows a space for signing and dating the contract.

the special conditions

The back page of the National contract form is headed with the address of the property being sold and the names of the parties and is devoted to the SPECIAL CONDITIONS OF SALE. These are similar to the ones on the Law Society's contract form.

Clause A will probably state that: "Condition 3 of the National Conditions of Sale shall not have effect". National condition 3 is similar to the Law Society general condition 4. It gives the buyer the right to rescind (that is to end) the contract by giving notice in writing to the seller or his solicitor within 16 days of the date of the contract, if he discovers any matter materially affecting the value of the property, except a matter which was not in existence at the time the contract was made, or a matter which he or his solicitor knew about when he entered into the contract. The buyer's right to rescind under National condition 3 is additional to his right to rescind under National condition 15, which will be explained in connection with clause D. For the same reasons as discussed earlier regarding Law Society general condition 4, most seller's solicitors will want to exclude National condition 3. If it is included, its effect can be limited by the filling in of the sentence in brackets: "But it shall not apply to a matter or matters affecting the value of the property by less than £—— or to the following ——". If National condition 3 is excluded from your contract, it means that you must not sign the contract until you have made thorough pre-contractual investigations.

Clause B begins: "Title shall be deduced and shall commence as follows:" Since you are buying registered land, the clause will be completed to read something like: "The vendor's title shall be deduced in accordance with section 110 of the Land Registration Act 1925". Section 110 governs how a seller proves his title to registered land. (Its requirements were outlined earlier when we looked at Law Society special condition E).

Clause C will state either that the property is sold with vacant possession or list details of any tenancies. If you are told that the property is sold subject to a tenancy, do not proceed without consulting a solicitor.

Clause D deals with planning law, under which you are not allowed to make changes in the use of property without planning permission. National condition 15 allows the buyer to ask questions (called 'requisitions') about the currently permitted use ('the authorised use') after exchange of contracts. But where a use is specified in clause D, the buyer has to accept it as the authorised use. On the other hand, the use being specified here means that the buyer can rescind the contract at any time before completion if he discovers that the specified use is not an authorised one.

Clause E is for use where certain items, for example furniture, are being sold separately to the buyer. A list of the items would have to be added to the contract together with the agreed price or the price set by a valuer, which would be additional to the price of the house, would appear here.

Clause F, finally will inform you of any restrictions the property is sold subject to, in much the same way as Matthew was told in clause G of his contract.

contract races

A solicitor acting for a seller may sometimes be instructed by his client to deal with more than one potential buyer at the same time, sending a draft contract to each, which can result in a race to exchange contracts. The practice is not viewed kindly by the legal profession and the council of the Law Society have said that the seller's solicitor must inform the buyer or his solicitor in writing whenever more than one draft contract has been sent out. Certain steps that Matthew takes after he receives his draft contract can be speeded up: for example, a personal search may be made at the local authority (although there are drawbacks to this procedure).

To speed things up, it is also possible to exchange contracts without making the appropriate searches and enquiries, or before obtaining your surveyor's report, and even before having your offer of a mortgage advance. The contract would then have to be made conditional on these matters having a satisfactory outcome (by inclusion into it of the Law Society optional general condition 4 or National condition 3). However if you are seriously contemplating this, you should consult a solicitor.

office copies of entries on the register and filed plan

Matthew now took up the office copies of the entries on the register and filed plan which Dodds & Son had sent him with the draft contract. Office copies are official photocopies prepared at the Land Registry; they state the district land registry they were issued from and the date on which they were made. They may be used as evidence in court proceedings and if a person suffers loss as a result of any inaccuracy in them he is entitled to be compensated by the Land Registry.

The register is the owner's proof of title. The purpose of sending office copies to the buyer or his solicitor is to fulfil, in part, the seller's obligation to prove his title – that is, to show that the property belongs to the seller and that he is able to transfer it to the buyer. (The task is completed by letting the buyer and his mortgagee have an authority to inspect the register). Technically, the seller's solicitor does not have to produce such evidence of title until contracts are exchanged. But since he does have to send to the buyer, with the draft contract, copies of any restrictions and other rights affecting the property, and these will normally be noted on the register, he invariably sends office copies of the whole of the title at this stage. This also saves him time and trouble later and can help to avoid delay in completion.

Some sellers' solicitors used merely to send photocopies of the land certificate or charge certificate as proof of title, instead of office copies. However, the council of the Law Society disapprove of this practice because ordinary photocopies may not show all the entries on the register and cannot be relied on in court proceedings. Additionally, when the sale is governed by the Law Society general conditions, condition 12(1)(b)(i) provides that copies of anything on the register or filed at the registry must be office copies.

This is what Matthew saw when he looked at the office copy of the entries on the Register which Dodds & Son had sent him:

H M LAND REGISTRY Map Reference ST4567L

TITLE NUMBER SY43271604

Edition 1 opened 4.7.60 This register consists of 2 pages

A. PROPERTY REGISTER

containing the description of the registered land and the estate comprised in the Title

---

COUNTY	DISTRICT
SURREY	MINFORD

The freehold land shown and edged with red on the plan of the above Title filed at the Registry registered on July 4, 1960 known as 14 Twintree Avenue

---

B. PROPRIETORSHIP REGISTER

stating nature of the Title, name, address and description of the proprietor of the land and any entries affecting the right of disposing thereof

TITLE ABSOLUTE

Entry Number	Proprietor etc
1	~~BERNARD SIMON ISAACS, Bus driver of 8 Ruddigore Road, Minford, Surrey. Price paid £400, registered on July 4 196~~0.
2	WILLIAM HERBERT TIMMS, Engineer, and MARGARET EDNA TIMMS his wife both of 15 Chapel Lane, Minford, Surrey registered on November 17, 1971
3	RESTRICTION registered on November 17, 1971: No disposition by one proprietor of the land (being the survivor of joint proprietors and not being a trust corporation) under which capital money arises is to be registered except under an order of the registrar or of the Court.

Any entries struck through in red are no longer subsisting.

Page 2 TITLE NUMBER SY43271604

C. CHARGES REGISTER

containing charges, incumbrances etc., adversely affecting the land and registered dealings therewith

Entry Number	The date at the beginning of each entry is the date on which the entry was made on this edition of the register	Application number and Remarks
1	July 4, 1960 – a transfer of the land in this title, dated June 14, 1960 by Minford Estates Developments Limited (Vendor) to Bernard Simon Isaacs (Purchaser) contains restrictive covenants. A copy of the covenants is set out in the schedule of restrictive covenants annexed hereto *The Schedule* 1. No further buildings shall be erected on the said land. 2. The land is not to be used for the purpose of carrying on the trade of business of an innkeeper or licensed victualler nor for a beer or spirit shop, or for the retail of any liquors and nothing is to be done or permitted on the land which may be or become a nuisance or annoyance to the adjoining houses or to the neighbourhood.	
2	November 17, 1971 – CHARGE dated November 1, 1971 registered on 17 November 1971 to secure the monies therein mentioned.	
	PROPRIETOR: THE MINFORD BUILDING SOCIETY of 102 Great Winchester Street, Minford, Surrey registered on 17 November 1971.	

Any entries struck through in red are no longer subsisting.

the three registers

The register of every property is divided into three parts:

the property register,
the proprietorship register, and
the charges register.

The first and last registers are sometimes described respectively as the 'credit' side (showing the estate and the benefit of any rights it enjoys) and 'debit' side (showing the burden of any incumbrances affecting it) of the register.

the property register

The property register contains a description of the property and the 'estate' for which it is held, that is, either freehold or leasehold. To complete the identification of the property the description usually refers to a filed plan, which is a separate individual plan drawn up for the particular title, showing the registered property outlined in red. Sometimes, in older titles, the land is described by reference to a section on the Land Registry's general map, which is the title plan for all the properties shown on it. This system has serious disadvantages and to-day filed plans are always used. Except where boundaries are noted as 'fixed', the filed plan indicates the general boundaries of the property only and cannot be used to determine disputes as to precise boundaries.

In some cases, the filed plan may show 'T' marks. The convention is that if the 'T' mark is on the inside of the boundary, the boundary is included in the property. The Land Registry only reproduce 'T' marks in two circumstances. One is where on an application for first registration the applicant insists that 'T' marks on a plan attached to the title deeds are put on to the filed plan. The other is where the 'T' marks are referred to in covenants contained in the deeds. You would find a mention of these covenants elsewhere on the register, and it might mean that you are under an obligation to maintain the boundary. In neither circumstance are the 'T' marks conclusive as to the exact ownership of the boundary.

If the property is leasehold, brief particulars of the lease are given including its date, who granted it, to whom, the date from when the lease runs and for how many years, and any ground rent payable. The register does not set out the lease in full, even though it is a very important document. However if you are buying a leasehold house you will be provided with a copy of the lease with the draft contract, and you should read this through carefully.

The property register also includes a description of any rights which go with the house, such as a right of way or right of drainage over another property. Such a right forms part of the property itself and it may constitute a valuable asset which enables the occupier to live in, or use the house more effectively. That is the reason for its registration in the property register.

Matthew checked the description in the property register and looked at the filed plan to make sure that it corresponded to the property he wanted to buy.

the proprietorship register

This contains details of:

- the nature of the registered title
- the name, address and description of the present registered owner of the property
- any restrictions that affect the registered owner's powers of dealing with the land
- cautions registered to protect a claim adverse to the title of the registered owner; and
- miscellaneous matters including bankruptcy inhibitions.

the nature of the registered title

When an application to register land for the first time is presented to the Land Registry, they not only investigate the applicant's title to the land but also award the title a class depending on its legal value. The class is then recorded on the register under the PROPRIETORSHIP REGISTER heading. A buyer can then tell from the register whether he is buying a 'perfect' title or, if not perfect, the type of defects that are likely to exist in the title.

The best class of title the registry can award is called TITLE ABSOLUTE and means that they are completely satisfied with the title that has been shown to them. Thereafter, the registered owner's title to the property is guaranteed, in the sense that it cannot be challenged except in very exceptional cases. And if such an exceptional case should arise and the registered owner is dispossessed, he would be entitled to be compensated by the Land Registry. 'Title absolute' can be awarded to both freehold and leasehold property.

If an applicant for first registration fails to satisfy the requirements of the Land Registry about title, and the Registry allows the applicant to register his title, it will not be with 'title absolute'. He will instead be given a lesser title; either 'good leasehold title', which applies to leaseholds only or 'possessory' or 'qualified' title which apply to both freeholds and leaseholds. This means that these lesser titles are only guaranteed from the date of first registration and the title before that date is not guaranteed and involves investigating in the same way as for unregistered land.

Thus, a freehold can be registered with one of three titles: title absolute or possessory title or qualified title. A leasehold, on the other hand, can be registered with one of four titles: title absolute or good leasehold title or possessory title or qualified title.

A buyer is advised not to proceed alone unless his seller is registered with 'title absolute'. If he encounters any one of the lesser titles, he should instruct a solicitor. Furthermore, building societies and other lenders are generally unwilling to lend money on the security of anything less than 'title absolute'.

description of the present owner

The proprietorship register will give the full name, address and usually the occupation of the registered owner.

Each time the property changes hands, the Land Registry adds the new owner's name to the proprietorship register and just strikes through the name of the previous owner – the seller. There is no need for the seller to prove title again nor the buyer to worry about it: when the Land Registry adds the new owner's name to the proprietorship register, they transfer the guarantee of title to the next owner. The proprietorship register often consists of a list of names and addresses, all but the last of which have been struck through. The name that is left is the name of the current registered proprietor.

A statement of the price paid for the property by an owner may also appear in this description. Because of this, the seller may snip the price out of the office copy he sends to the buyer and not hand the snippet over until after exchange of contracts, when the buyer has legally committed himself to a price. Otherwise the buyer might be influenced in deciding what price he should pay. For property that has been sold since 1976, the Land Registry has followed this practice and omitted the price, so in many cases entries will not include the price.

Matthew verified from the proprietorship register that Mr and Mrs Timms were the registered proprietors with 'TITLE ABSOLUTE'.

restrictions

Any limitations on a registered owner's powers of dealing with the property must be recorded on the proprietorship register by an entry called a restriction. A registered owner is deemed to have full power to do what he likes with his land unless such an entry states otherwise.

Matthew noticed that a restriction had been entered against Mr and Mrs Timms: the survivor of them could not sell (or for that matter lease or mortgage) 14 Twintree Avenue without an order of the registrar or the court. This told Matthew that the Timms owned the property jointly as beneficial tenants-in-common.

co-ownership

Since 1925 all concurrent ownership of land by joint tenants or tenants-in-common has to exist behind what is known as a trust for sale. This is a legal device whereby the co-owners (husband and wife, or any other two or more persons) hold the legal title in the property on trust for themselves and although the trust is to sell, the co-owners may postpone sale indefinitely.

As far as the tenants themselves and the outside world are concerned, there is no difference between a joint tenancy and tenancy-in-common while co-ownership continues. The distinction occurs mainly on death.

Joint tenants do not have a specific share or defined interest in the property, each owns the whole jointly with the other. So, when one of the joint tenants dies, his interest in the property automatically vests in the other, irrespective of anything in the will of the dead joint tenant; the will is irrelevant for this purpose. Because of this 'rule of survivorship' the surviving joint tenant has the whole of the interest in the property himself, and like any other absolute owner has full power to deal with it as he likes, including selling it, and can give a valid receipt to the buyer for the purchase money. There is therefore no need for a restriction to be entered on the proprietorship register where property is beneficially owned by joint tenants.

Tenants-in-common, on the other hand, do have a specific share in the property – one-half, a third or whatever – and are free to deal with that share as they please. When one tenant-in-common dies, his share passes under his will or on his intestacy and not necessarily to the surviving owner. Because the rule of survivorship has no application to a tenancy-in-common, it is impossible to say without further evidence that on the death of one tenant-in-common the survivor is entitled to the whole interest in the property. A restriction on the proprietorship register is needed to warn the buyer that the survivor cannot give a valid receipt for the purchase money without which the buyer would not get good title. (And on a sale of the house while both 'tenants' are alive, both must sign – execute – the transfer deed.)

other reasons for restrictions

Another example of the use of a restriction occurs in the case of what is called settled land, where the proprietor (the tenant for life) is entitled to the land for his life only and it then passes to others, the 'remaindermen', after his death. The tenant for life will be the registered proprietor (with 'absolute' title if the title is

OK), but to protect the interests of the remaindermen, a restriction will be entered in the proprietorship register to the effect that the land can only be dealt with in the manner authorised by the Settled Land Act. This includes sale, but any proceeds of sale must be paid to at least two named trustees of the settlement, to ensure that the tenant for life does not abscond with the money.

A restriction will also be used where the registered proprietor is a company whose rules limit its powers in relation to land or where certain land cannot be transferred without the consent of, for example, the Charity Commissioners.

The idea behind restrictions is really quite simple. If there are none entered on the proprietorship register, you are entitled to assume that the registered owner has full power to deal with the property (except for any 'overriding interests'). If on the other hand there is a restriction, all you have to do is comply with its terms in order to get good title to the land.

cautions

The entry of a caution is essentially a 'hostile action' and a short term measure. It can be used by someone who has a claim to the land adverse to the title of the registered proprietor. The consent of the registered proprietor is unnecessary.

Once a caution against dealings has been entered on the proprietorship register, no dealing with the property, such as selling or mortgaging, by the registered proprietor will be registered until the person who lodged the caution (the cautioner) has been given notice of it and had a chance to object.

Examples of the type of interests protected by a caution are a claim by someone else to be the rightful owner of the property, or the rights of another buyer under a contract for sale, if the seller has been two-timing you (perhaps the seller has earlier exchanged contracts with another buyer – unlikely, but it can happen).

From the buyer's point of view, a caution acts as a warning to 'beware' before completing his purchase. You need not enquire of the seller as to its cause but you must insist on his procuring its removal from the register before completion, or that the cautioner's consent to the sale is obtained.

miscellaneous entries
Most important under this head are creditor's notices and bankruptcy inhibitions. If you find either of these entries on the proprietorship register, do not proceed without consulting a solicitor. (If you ignore the warning and go ahead and buy, you would probably not get good title.)

the charges register

This part of the register contains details of rights which other people have over or in respect of the property, and which (except in the case of a mortgage) will continue to bind the property irrespective of who owns it. They are rights and interests which detract from, or take something away from, the owner's property as described in the property register and are often referred to as incumbrances.

The three most important kinds are restrictive covenants, mortgages and the rights of a spouse to occupy the matrimonial home.

Restrictive covenants are an important feature of conveyancing. Where a landowner sells of a large piece of land which is to be turned into a housing estate, he usually requires the developer to undertake that certain conditions shall in future be complied with; for example, he may insist that not more than so many houses to the acre should be built on the land. Likewise the developer, when he comes to sell off the new houses to the first owners, may require each of them to undertake that the houses should not be turned into a shop, or that no new building be built on the land without the consent of the developer. In both cases, these restrictions are made in the form of written covenants set out in the deed that transfers the property from the seller to the buyer. The buyer is said to enter into restrictive covenants with the seller and the object is usually that this should be done in such a way that not only the first buyer but all subsequent owners should be bound by the covenants. Normally the covenants are quite reasonable and unlikely to prevent a buyer from doing anything he wants to do with the property. They can be of advantage to the individual house owners, because they generally operate throughout the neighbourhood.

There is some uncertainty in legal circles about just how far restrictive covenants can be enforced when the property has changed hands. However, a house buyer should assume that all the covenants set out in the charges register can be enforced against him when he becomes the owner.

If you find the restrictive covenants which affect your proposed new house unpalatable or unacceptable, you should consult a solicitor (or look for another property).

Restrictive covenants are 'noted' on the charges register. The deeds which contain them are listed and the covenants themselves are then set out in full in a schedule.

Mortgages on the other hand are generally 'registered' in the charges register. There is an entry in two parts for each mortgage. The first states the date of the charge and of registration, and the second states the name of the owner of the charge, the building society or other lender. Make sure that they are crossed out after completion.

A spouse's rights of occupation are protected by the entry of a notice on the charges register. The rights are given by the Matrimonial Homes Act 1983 (which consolidated the earlier Matrimonial Homes Act 1967 and subsequent amendments) to a spouse (husband or wife) who is not the registered proprietor, and are: if in occupation, not to be evicted from the matrimonial home solely owned by the other spouse; or, if not in occupation, to go into occupation under an order of the court.

Once protected by a notice on this part of the register, the rights are binding on a buyer from the spouse/registered proprietor. In other words, if you bought the house, the seller's spouse would still have the right to go on living there. If you find such a notice, you must require the seller to get it cancelled before completion.

The charges register of 14 Twintree Avenue involved Matthew in a little more reading than the other two parts had done. None of the restrictive covenants listed in the schedule seemed troublesome to him: he was not intending to open a beerhouse. He noted that entries 2 and 3 related to the Timms' existing mortgage. This would have to be paid off when Matthew's purchase was completed, and he would have to make sure that the Minford Building Society would not have any right to claim that the house was still mortgaged to them once it had become his property.

Finally he noted that the office copies had been "issued by Tunbridge Wells District Land Registry showing the subsisting entries on the register on 10 January 1986".

It had taken Matthew a good part of saturday to read through the draft contract and office copies. He heaved a sigh of relief and put the office copies away in his file; he would need these when making his 'requisitions on title' after exchange of contracts.

Before he could approve the draft contract, he would need to have the answers to certain enquiries he would make of the seller and the local authority.

enquiries before contract

A sale of land often produces a conflict of interests. A buyer naturally wants to find out all he can about the property, good or bad, whereas a seller, while willing to sing its praises, may not be so keen to disclose its faults.

buyer beware

The general rule, known as the *caveat emptor* (buyer beware) rule in the law of contract, is that a seller is under no duty to disclose material facts to a prospective buyer. In other words, the buyer enters into the contract at his own risk. This *caveat emptor* rule applies also to sales of land, but with one exception: the seller must inform the buyer of any latent defects in his title. These are incumbrances and other adverse matters of title which the buyer could not discover by himself even if he undertakes a reasonable inspection of the property itself. An example would be the restrictive covenants on 14 Twintree Avenue we have just looked at, which is why Dodds & Son mentioned them in the draft contract and sent an office copy to Matthew. But the seller is under no duty to disclose patent defects in title. These are third-party rights of which there is some visible indication on the property and so can be discovered on inspection – such as a path running across land signposted 'public right of way'.

The Law Society general condition 5(1) additionally requires the seller to disclose any patent easements and other rights of which he knows or ought to know, other than those known to the buyer at the date of the contract or which a prudent purchaser would have discovered by that date. This condition does not significantly add to what is said above. A prudent buyer is expected to inspect the property. If the easement right is not capable of being discovered by a prudent buyer's inspection, then it is arguably a latent defect in title – and should be disclosed anyway.

Neither need a seller disclose any physical defect in the property, latent or patent (a latent physical defect might be a damaged flue; a patent physical defect, a missing chimney). But if he does say something about the quality of the property and this turns out to be untrue after exchange of contracts, it may amount to a misrepresentation entitling the buyer to end the contract and/or claim damages.

Because of the *caveat emptor* rule, the buyer's solicitor has always presented the seller's solicitor with a list of questions about the property, before contracts were exchanged. These 'enquiries before contract' or 'preliminary enquiries' are now usually made on a standard form, with any particular enquiries added and (occasionally) inappropriate enquiries struck out.

form Conveyancing 29 (Long)

To make his enquiries, Matthew used the same printed form as most solicitors do: Oyez's ENQUIRIES BEFORE CONTRACT, *Conveyancing 29 (Long)*. The form is frequently revised to improve its usage and keep up to date with new developments in the law and practice. It is therefore important for you to obtain the most recent version of the form. (At the time of going to press in February 1986, this is "revised April 1985".)

The first 12 questions under the heading GENERAL ENQUIRIES apply to all properties and deal with such subjects as ownership and maintenance of boundaries; disputes (with neighbours, in particular); guarantees (such as for dry rot treatment) and any claims settled or pending under them; main services (supply of water, gas, electricity); facilities enjoyed by the seller, alone or with others (such as a joint driveway) and their maintenance; occupation by persons other than the seller; restrictive covenants, planning, outgoings on the property and when and how completion is to take place. We shall deal with what type of matters these questions are likely to reveal and their importance to the buyer a little later on when Matthew receives his replies.

The thirteenth question on the form, "New Properties", applies only to newly-built houses and covers some of the particular problems that arise in such cases.

If you find a question 13 dealing with development land tax, ignore it. It means that you have an old form Conveyancing 29 (Long).

Then follows a blank space for any additional questions. In the case of a straightforward sale of an owner-occupied house which has a registered title, extra enquiries are rarely made and generally to be discouraged. They can cause unnecessary delay and expense. In less simple cases, however, especially with unregistered land, points may occur to the buyer's solicitor on which he needs extra information or assurance.

The back of the form lists five questions which apply to leasehold property only. These deal with

- whether the lease is a head lease (one where the lessor owns the freehold) or an underlease (where the lessor himself owns the property under a lease, out of which the present lease is carved, granted by a superior lessor who usually owns the freehold)
- the names and addresses of the various lessors, their respective solicitors, and the agents (if any) to whom any rent is paid
- past licences given by the lessor, for example for alterations to be carried out

- where a lessor's consent is necessary for a sale, what steps have been taken to obtain this
- whether the seller or his lessor has broken any covenants in the lease (a lease contains various obligations, called covenants, which have to be observed by both lessor and lessee)
- whether the requirements in the lease about painting and doing other work have been honoured.

Question III regarding service charges is likely to be inapplicable to a leasehold house. The form goes on to ask for details of insurance, which under the terms of the lease may have to be placed with a particular insurance company; and whether or not there are, with the deeds, office copies of the lessor's title (this will either be the freehold title or any superior lease).

A space is left for additional enquiries. There is one additional enquiry that the buyer of a leasehold house might usefully ask. The Leasehold Reform Act 1967 entitles certain lessees of houses to buy their freeholds or claim extended leases. To qualify under the Act the lessee must satisfy the following conditions:

- he must have a lease of a house, for a term exceeding 21 years
- he must have occupied the house as his only or main residence for the whole of the last 3 years or for a total of three out of the last 10 years and during the period of qualifying residence the rent must have been less than two-thirds of the rateable value of the property
- the rateable value must be within certain limits.

Your local valuation officer will help with rateable values. The procedure (fully described in the Consumer Publication *Renting and letting*) for buying the freehold or getting an extended lease begins by the lessee serving a notice on the lessor claiming one or other of his rights under the Act. The buyer of a lease of a house which qualifies under the Act should therefore ask, by way of an additional enquiry, how long the seller has been resident in the house and whether he has served a notice on the lessor purporting to exercise his rights under the 1967 Act, and if so, whether he will pass the benefit of the notice to the buyer.

supplementary enquiries before contract

Matthew, being a first-time buyer and inexperienced at becoming an owner-occupier, felt he wanted more information about 14 Twintree Avenue than the standard enquiries would divulge. He decided to take advantage of the set of extra questions Oyez now provide on form Con 29 (Supplementary) to accompany their basic enquiries. The five questions on the form SUPPLEMENTARY ENQUIRIES BEFORE CONTRACT delve more deeply into the condition of the house, the services, any garage and parking restrictions, chattels and fixtures and various financial details. Again, we shall discuss the questions in more detail when Matthew receives his answers.

Matthew's enquiries

At the top of the form Conveyancing 29 (Long), Matthew wrote in *14 Twintree Avenue, Minford, Surrey*. Underneath was a space for writing the name of the seller and buyer. Matthew needed answers to all but the last of the general enquiries (question 13 is relevant to new properties only). He therefore crossed out question 13 and the leasehold enquiries which were, of course, inapplicable. He then attached the supplementary enquiries to the form and signed and dated it, ready to post on monday to Dodds & Son. He would need to post them in duplicate, so he filled in copies of both the forms, identically, to send with a covering letter.

38 Broadstone Drive
Hastings, Sussex

To: Messrs Dodds & Son

20 January 1986

Dear Sirs,

Re: 14 Twintree Avenue, Minford

Thank you for your letter of 16 January enclosing a draft contract in duplicate relating to my proposed purchase of the above property, and office copies of the entries on the register and filed plan.

I enclose some preliminary enquiries, with a copy.

Yours faithfully,

M. J. Seaton

local searches

That same weekend Matthew prepared, for despatch early monday morning, an application for a local land charges search and also enquiries to the local authority.

A local search is an application for an official certificate showing the entries on the local land charges register, at the date of the search. Every local authority has to keep a register of local land charges, from which a buyer of property within the area can discover any obligations (called land charges) which the local authority can enforce against successive owners of property under the terms of various acts of parliament. Generally speaking, a local land charge can be any matter of a public nature affecting land; some are charges in the ordinary sense, involving the payment of money, others restrict or limit the ways in which land can be used – or, in the case of compulsory acquisition, prevent its use altogether or in part. All promote public welfare (for example, a tree preservation order) as opposed to benefiting an individual. Local land charges are usually in favour of or imposed by a local authority or other public body, such as a water authority. The authority which brings the charge into existence is under a duty to register it with the appropriate council.

From the buyer's point of view, a local land charge is important because it will be enforceable against him when he becomes the new owner of the property. This is true even if the charge is not registered or, if registered, even if the buyer's local search does not reveal the existence of the charge. A buyer who suffers loss in either of these cases is, however, entitled to compensation – but only if he makes a local land charges search in the proper manner.

A local land charges search may reveal two types of charge, financial and/or restrictive.

Financial charges come into existence because various statutes, such as the Highways or Public Health Acts, empower local authorities to recover from owners of property the cost of executing certain works. Suppose, for example, that a local authority has to remove a rubbish tip which has become a danger to health from the garden of a private house: the cost of removing the tip becomes a charge on the house. As with a mortgage, if the local authority is not reimbursed, they can sell the house to pay their debt.

If the buyer's search reveals a financial charge he must insist, by making it a condition of the contract, that it will be paid off before completion. Alternatively, the buyer should get an appropriate reduction in the purchase price of the property, to offset the fact that he will be responsible for paying off the charge when he becomes the new proprietor.

Restrictive charges range from an order listing a building as one of special architectural or historic interest to an order requiring a landowner to stop the spread of injurious weeds. A buyer like Matthew would, however, be more likely to come across an order designating Minford as a smoke control area. This would mean that he could burn only smokeless fuel and he would have to check that any appliances at 14 Twintree Avenue were suitable for this purpose. Or he might discover that a new improvement line had been made for Twintree Avenue: that the Minford council had decided to widen the road to ease the flow of traffic. This could mean that Matthew's new house would lose part of the garden and he would have to decide whether to proceed with his purchase at the agreed price, or at all. If the house had been near an opencast coal mine or civil airport, a local land charge may have been registered giving the National Coal Board or Civil Aviation Authority the right compulsorily to acquire the property or to enter onto it to maintain power cables or other equipment they had installed there.

Needless to say, a prospective buyer is usually anxious to receive the results of his local land charges search. But it is important to realise that a search certificate speaks only as to the state of affairs on the day of its date. After that date, a change may occur that alters the whole picture.

local land charges search

A local search is made with the local district council or appropriate borough council. In Matthew's case, it was Minford District Council. He used form LLC1 (*Register of local land charges,*

Requisition for search and official certificate of search). He wrote the name and address of the Minford District Council in the space at the top of the form.

Form LLC1 has a printed duplicate of itself attached, to be torn off and retained by the local council, the original only being sent back with the signed certificate on it. Both parts must be filled in.

The register of local land charges is divided into 12 parts and a buyer may apply for a search in just those parts with which he is concerned. The almost universal practice is to apply for a search of the whole register, which is what Matthew did. To achieve this he crossed out the words "*Parts . . . of*" on the form to make it read: "An official search is required in the register of local land charges".

In filling in the form it is seldom necessary to do more than describe the property by its address: in Matthew's case, 14 Twintree Avenue, Minford, Surrey was sufficient. Where the property can only be identified by a plan, a copy of the plan should be sent with the form.

Matthew signed the form and wrote his name, address and telephone number in the panel provided. The fees for obtaining a local land charges search certificate are stated on the form (£2.90 in Matthew's case).

A local land charges search usually takes a few weeks to process. To save time, a local search may be made in person with the appropriate district council. However, it is easy to miss charges that have been registered and a buyer who makes his own search will not be entitled to compensation if he overlooks an entry which has been properly recorded by the council. Moreover, district councils do not encourage personal searches; it strains their resources.

enquiries of local authorities

With form LLC1 Matthew would send an application for answers to a number of enquiries of the local authority.

There are two forms for this. Con.29A *Enquiries of District Councils* (white) is for use in the whole of England and Wales excluding London. Form Con.29D *Enquiries of Local Authority* (buff) is for use in respect of properties in the area of London borough councils or the Corporation of London.

Whereas a local search reveals particular public matters affecting a property, these enquiries offer a buyer a more general view of what is going on in the area: they give details of such matters as roads, drains and sewers, planning and conservation.

The form is divided into two parts. Part I contains 18 questions which will be answered automatically by the local authority. There is a fee for obtaining replies to all the enquiries in Part I (at present £10.60). Part II contains 13 optional enquiries. Replies will only be given to those Part II enquiries against which the buyer places his initials, and pays the cost of obtaining a reply (at present 80p per enquiry). It is also possible to add additional enquiries to those on the form (present fee £2 per additional enquiry).

The significance of many of the enquiries on the form (and the replies to them) is not easy to appreciate, so we have grouped the enquiries most likely to concern a d-i-y buyer under subject headings.

roads

Question 1 relates to roads and footpaths and will inform you whether you are likely to incur any expense in their maintenance. (The county council which is usually the highway authority for its area is obliged to keep a register of highways maintainable at the public expense.) Thus, 1A asks whether the roads etc. are maintainable at the public expense, and 1B whether the council has passed a resolution to make up the road fronting the property at the expense of the frontagers. The box for the description of the property, on the front of the form, has a space in which the enquirer is invited to enter details of roads etc. to which question 1 is to relate, in addition to the road given in the address. You should therefore wait until you have a plan of the property, before sending off your enquiries; the plan will show you whether there is a return road frontage or even a rear accessway or passageway of which you should check the maintenance responsibilities.

Question 2 also relates to roads but will reveal whether the council has any future proposals for road construction or improvement nearby, which could interfere with your enjoyment of the property. Very few buyers want a new motorway or bypass at the bottom of their garden.

Local authorities have the power to close or divert a road or path. Optional enquiry II in part II of the form asks whether the local authority has approved any proposals for the stopping up or diversion of any roads or paths referred to on the front of the form, and is worth initialling by the buyer. Such proposals may affect access to the property on a permanent or temporary basis.

notices

Question 3 asks for details of any outstanding or informal notices issued by the council under the Public Health Acts, Housing Acts or Highways Act. You might discover from the answer to this question that the seller has been told to repair faulty guttering or carry out other compulsory repairs to the house, or that the roads adjacent to the house are to be widened, or that other development is to be carried out on or near the property.

building regulations

Question 4 asks whether the local authority have started proceedings for breach of building regulations in respect of the property. Building regulations lay down certain minimum standards which must be complied with when a new house is built or an old one altered. They control such things as structural fire precautions, thermal and sound insulation, damp-proofing, ventilation, the size of windows and the height of rooms. Contravention of building regulations is a criminal offence and the owner of the property may have to remove or alter the offending works. If the answer to question 4 is "yes" the buyer should require the seller to remedy the breach before completion, or ask for a reduction in the purchase price so that he can carry out the necessary works after completion.

sewers

Question 5 is similar to the first question on roads. The reply will tell you whether the sewers and drains serving the property are maintainable at public expense or whether you must pay the cost of connecting the property up to, or maintaining, sewer facilities. The importance of the reply should not be underestimated. A buyer who has to contribute towards the cost of a private sewer or drain may find that he has assumed a heavy financial responsibility. A defective private drain or sewer may amount to a nuisance in law, and the local authority or a neighbour can compel the owner to carry out remedial works.

planning

Questions 6 and 11 relate to planning. The reply to question 6 will disclose whether the property is free from enforcement proceedings regarding planning. Where something is done in breach of planning control, the local authority may issue an 'enforcement notice'. This could be because a condition attached to a planning permission has not been complied with, or because the necessary planning permission was not applied for in the first place. Basically, planning permission is needed for major building work or changing the use of the property. An enforcement notice specifies the breach of planning control, the action which must be taken to remedy the breach (this could even mean taking the building down) and the time within which this must be done. Failure to comply with an enforcement notice is a criminal offence. Furthermore, in the event of non-compliance, the local authority can enter on to the property and carry out the remedial works themselves. The cost is charged to the current owner of the property, whether or not he was the one who broke planning control. If you discover that an enforcement notice has been issued in respect of the house you want to buy, you should insist that the seller complies with it before completion or that the purchase price is adjusted to take account of the fact that you will have to do the remedial works after completion.

An enforcement notice can be appealed against. An appeal can take some time to determine, and where works are in progress, the local authority will back up their enforcement notice with a 'stop notice'. A stop notice has the effect of maintaining the status quo (building work must be discontinued) until the outcome of the appeal is known.

Every local planning authority keeps a register (open to public inspection) of enforcement proceedings relating to land in its area, after 27 November 1981. That means any enforcement or stop notices issued after that date will be noted (earlier ones will be revealed by the buyer's local land charges search). The reply to question 6 will state where the register of enforcement and stop notices can be inspected.

Every local planning authority must also keep a register of planning applications made in the area, and the results. Enquiry 11 will tell you whether any entries relating to the property have been made in this register and where it can be inspected. An inspection of this register is recommended: it will forewarn you of any pending development in the area, for example a planned but not yet built supermarket, and it will reveal the local planning authority's probable attitude towards any changes you are intending to make to the property.

long-term planning

Enquiry 7 asks about structure and local plans. A *structure plan* is a written statement, approved by the Secretary of State, of a county council's (or London borough council's) broad planning policy for its area. It outlines the physical and economic characteristics of the area, deals with population size and distribution, and shows plans for industry, transportation, housing and other matters such as conservation. A *local plan* is drawn up by a district council (or metropolitan borough). It is similar in style to a structure plan, but it does not need the approval of the Secretary of State, and develops in detail the broad policies of the structure plan for its district. If, for example, the structure plan says that light industry should be encouraged, the local plan will relate this policy to a particular site.

The information given in reply to question 7 will include the stage reached in the preparation of either plan, and whether any proposals to alter an existing plan have been made public and, in the case of a local plan, whether the area in which the property is situated has been given a primary use, such as residential or commercial.

smokeless zones
The answer to question 16 will inform you whether the area is shortly to become a smoke-control area in which it is an offence for smoke to be emitted from a chimney.

listed buildings and conservation areas
If you buy a house which is architecturally or historically important (a listed building) or in a conservation area, your freedom to alter it may be restricted (over and above the need to apply for planning permission). Your local land charges search will reveal whether the property is already listed and the reply to question 13 whether it is likely to be listed in the near future. Question 12 relates to conservation areas.

tree preservation orders
Question 9 asks whether the local authority has resolved to make a tree preservation order in respect of the property. Once an order has been made it is an offence to cut down, top, lop or uproot the specified tree(s) without the consent of the local authority. The order itself is registerable as a local land charge and will show up on the buyer's local land charges search. Question 9 forewarns a buyer that such an order will be made.

compulsory acquisition and slum clearance
Enquiry 14 will reveal whether the local authority has plans to compulsorily acquire the property. No buyer should buy a property which is about to be compulsorily acquired. Enquiry 15 asks if the property is in a slum clearance area. If it is, it is very likely to be compulsorily acquired at some time in the future.

pipelines
If you are planning to extend your property, enquiry VIII in part II should be asked (by putting your initials against it on the form). This will reveal the proximity of pipelines to the property. Where there is a pipeline, you are not allowed to put up any building or structure within 10 feet of the surface of the land over the pipeline, without permission.

Matthew filled in Con.29A asking for replies to the part I enquiries and enquiries II and VIII (he was thinking of building a greenhouse) of the part II ones.

On monday, Matthew would send both forms to Minford District Council at the council offices. He enclosed a cheque, payable to Minford District Council, for £15.10. (Because some local authorities sometimes introduce charges at different levels, it is best to check with the authority what the cost is.)

A local authority can take as little as about two weeks to return the local land charges search certificate and replies to enquiries (but some, particularly London boroughs, sometimes take considerably longer).

Having to wait for search forms to be completed by the council can delay the purchase of your house more than anything else. Therefore, even if you are going to make a personal visit to the council, unless you plan to do so within a few days of receiving the draft contract, send the forms to the council as soon as the draft contract arrives.

When carrying out your local enquiries by sending the appropriate forms to your local council, for the local land charges search the council sends back an official certificate of search, and the enquiries are usually answered by the council attaching to the form a standard printed form of answers. If you are going to carry out a personal local search, you will be given written or oral answers, or a mixture of both.

personal local search

It is possible to make the local enquiries in person to the local authority.

If you are trying to get your conveyance through especially quickly, it is possible to proceed on the basis of a personal search alone, to speed things up. For the purposes of obtaining a mortgage, the building society solicitor will require an official search eventually. There is a real risk if you exchange contracts on the basis of a personal search and something is revealed by the official result later, that the building society might refuse the loan and then you would not have the funds to comply with your contract.

And remember: if you suffer loss because the local authority misses something they ought not to have, they must compensate you if the enquiries were made by post. No such protection applies, however, if you make what turns out to be inadequate enquiries in person.

Advantages of carrying out a personal search are:

- You may pick up information about the property through the personal touch: someone at the council might say "You do realise that Elm Grove carries heavy traffic in summer don't you?"
- planning application for adjoining property is not covered by the local search form, so you can ask about that when you do a personal search
- proposed new roads or redevelopment do not show on a local search form until they are at a stage where they are put on one of the council's registers, therefore ask about this (whether you do a personal search or not)

before you go to the council for a personal search

1. Make sure you know which council to go to. Phone to check, if you have any doubt (ask for 'local land charges') or 'local enquiries'. If you are buying in London it is quickest to phone County Hall (01-633 5000) and they will tell you, for instance, whether a property in SE19 comes under Croydon or Southwark Borough Council.
2. Ask if you may do a personal search, give them the description of the property (the address is usually sufficient), make an appointment and find out who to ask for when you get there. The council needs to know when you are coming so they can do their homework and preparation.
3. Fill in the forms, putting the full address of the council at the top of each form, the description (address of the property you are buying) and your name and address where indicated. The forms must also be signed and dated.

Using form 29A or 29D is not obligatory and if you are going to do a personal search for a property for which a mortgage is not required, you can compile your own list of questions. It is useful to have a list of any extra questions with you in any case.

Written answers are not supplied at a personal search to part II enquiries (which used to be called 'additional enquiries' and still are in conversation, for example with the council). Some councils will not permit oral answers to additional enquiries, but some will.

4. Attach a plan of the property in duplicate to form LLC1 if there is anything less than straightforward about the house, for example, if the garage is separate or the house stands in its own large grounds. If this is the case, the curtilage (area attached to the house as part of its enclosure) will have to be searched.

5. Have your money ready. A personal search costs £1.15. A complete official search costs £13.50. (You can pay by cheque.)

on the day of the personal search

If you start in the local land charges department when you arrive at the council, form LLC1 can be dealt with there. Some boroughs' local land charges departments will accept form LLC1 from you in person but only for later return by post. Some will complete it while you wait, if they can.

You may be given a printed form with the standard replies to your enquiries on form Con29A or D at the outset and some directions about where to obtain the non-standard replies, and you will be directed to the appropriate departments. It may take you only about half an hour to get all the information you need if all the departments are in one open plan office; a little longer if the departments are in different parts of a complex building. Or you may be told, when you phone, that getting all your replies will take half a day because the departments are in a number of places.

The advantage of a personal search is speed. But a personal search confers no protection against negligent replies from the local authority or unrevealed local land charges.

replies to enquiries before contract

Dodds & Son sent back Matthew's enquiries before contract with their replies quite quickly.

DODDS & SON
Solicitors

1 Charter Street
Minford, Surrey

24 January 1986

Dear Sir,

Re: 14 Twintree Avenue

We enclose our answers to your preliminary enquiries and look forward to hearing from you with the draft contract duly approved as soon as possible.

Yours faithfully,

Dodds & Son

Some sellers' solicitors give non-committal and meaningless replies to preliminary enquiries. They are afraid of making inaccurate representations about the property which may result in the sale being frustrated: misrepresentation may entitle the buyer to rescind the contract (and/or claim damages from the seller) and solicitors fear being liable in negligence to either the seller or the buyer or both. However, the current trend amongst good solicitors, encouraged by the council of the Law Society, is to be as helpful and informative as possible, which indeed Dodds & Son had been.

boundaries

The first question on the form *Conveyancing 29 (Long)* concerned the ownership and maintenance of boundary walls, fences, hedges and ditches. Ownership and maintenance of boundaries do not necessarily go hand in hand. The answer referred to a plan, included with the replies, which was drawn at the time the house was first sold, in 1960. The convention of putting 'T' marks on the inside of boundary lines on plans is to indicate which boundaries belong to the property. From the plan it appeared that two of the fences belonged to 14 Twintree Avenue (the two with the 'T' marks on the inside), but there was nothing to say that Matthew would be obliged to maintain them. Such an obligation only arises where there is an express covenant to maintain certain fences, etc. (this covenant would be noted on the proprietorship register). So Matthew could not be forced to maintain his fences. The 'T' marks on the 1960 plan had not been copied onto the filed plan of 14 Twintree Avenue because the Land Registry did not start noting 'T' marks (even if they were referred to in the deeds or an applicant for first registration insisted) until after 1962.

Except where it is noted on the property register that the boundaries have been fixed, the filed plan indicates general boundaries only and cannot be used in a boundary dispute.

The Consumer Publication *Householder's action guide* includes a section dealing with the presumptions which apply if no definite evidence exists as to ownership of boundaries.

disputes and notices

Question 2 was about disputes. This is important for a buyer. No one wants to buy a house and find himself involved in a legal wrangle. Question 2B was specially designed to give the buyer as much advance warning as possible about potential trouble with neighbours. It asked the seller whether during the past three years he had complained or had cause to complain about the state of repair or use of neighbouring property. Dodds & Son had written "no" against both 2A and 2B. The 'three years' has no special legal significance, the period is arbitrarily chosen. If the seller had had a dispute with his neighbour four years previously, but that had been put right and he had no further cause to complain, the answer would be "no"; it need only be other than "no" if there had been trouble during the preceding three years.

Question 3 related to notices; there were none. Notices concerning both public and private matters might be revealed in answer to this question. One of the enquiries the buyer makes of the local authority is whether any informal notice has been issued in respect of the property. If the reply states that a notice has been issued it will say where it may be inspected, but may not give further details. The seller, who will have been served with the notice, should provide the buyer with a copy of it in reply to question 3. In the last resort, the buyer will have to inspect the notices at the local authority's offices.

Examples of notices relating to private actions include a writ served by or against a neighbour for private nuisance, or a notice of claim served on the National House Building Council.

guarantees

The question about guarantees asked for copies of such documents as the agreement or certificate or insurance policy issued by, for example, the National House Building Council for a house built or converted under their scheme, or woodworm treatment guarantees, or agreements relating to roads or footpaths (this would apply more to a house in a new development, but even for a second-hand house which abuts a private road, there may be an agreement with neighbouring proprietors as to maintenance). A buyer should be concerned to get the benefit of such guarantees. Information is requested about them now, so that on completion they can be transferred to the newcomer. This can be by simple letter from the seller to the buyer saying: "In consideration of your completing the purchase of my house, I now assign to you the benefit of the guarantee etc. dated XYZ which I received from AB regarding CD and E." A copy of the letter of assignment should be sent to the people who gave the guarantee. The benefit of a National House Building Council's agreement does not need to be expressly transferred to the buyer.

Question 4 also asks whether any claim has been made or settled under any of the guarantees. If you are the second or later buyer of a house built or converted under the NHBC scheme whose protection lasts for 10 years (7 for a conversion) it is important for you to check that the seller has given prompt notice in writing of any defect to the builder (for up to two years after the house was built or converted) or to the Council (during the 2–10 or 2–7 year period). The benefits of the scheme depend on prompt notice of claims. The buyer should also get the seller to promise (by adding a special condition in the contract) to notify the builder or the Council of any defects which appear between the return of form *Conveyancing 29 Long* and completion.

services and facilities

Question 5A asked whether the property had drainage, electricity, gas and other main services (they were connected), and 5B whether the water supply was metered (it was not). Most of us pay for our water as a percentage of the general rate. Metered water supply is financially advantageous to someone who uses up little water, or who lives in a house with a very high rateable value.

Where a property has, for example, a private water supply or drainage facilities, it is sometimes necessary to lay pipes or drains in somebody else's land. 5C and D ask for details of this and for the route of the pipes etc. and for copies of any documents authorising their use. A buyer needs to know that he will be able to continue to enjoy the benefit of these facilities. However non-discovery is not fatal. The benefit of such rights passes automatically to the buyer in the deed transferring the property, without the need for specific mention.

But non-discovery of a water-abstraction licence, referred to in 5E, could be serious to the buyer of a country property. Suppose the property gets its water supply from a local stream: the consent of the relevant water authority is needed to abstract water from an inland source. If the property has the benefit of a water abstraction licence, this will pass automatically to the buyer on completion but he will lose the licence if he does not inform the appropriate water authority within one month of completion that he has become the new owner of the property.

Question 6 asked about facilities, either enjoyed by the property exclusively or in common with anyone else (other than facilities referred to in question 5). There were none in Matthew's case, but an example of the former might be a fire escape serving the property alone; of the latter, a joint driveway.

adverse rights and overriding interests

Broadly speaking, overriding interests are third-party interests in registered land which will bind a buyer of the land notwithstanding that they are not recorded on the register and notwithstanding that the buyer has no actual knowledge of their existence. They are an exception to the basic principle of registered land, that all matters relevant to title are shown on the register. The justification for this seems to be that overriding interests, in the main, are rights which any buyer can easily discover if he bothers to go and look at the property he is intending to buy.

A list of overriding interests is contained in section 70(1) of the Land Registration Act 1925. The most important ones likely to affect a buyer are informal rights of way and similar rights, leases of under 21 years (which are not capable of being protected by registration), squatters' rights, and the rights of every person in actual occupation.

One point to remember, as a buyer of registered land, is that you do not become the legal owner of the property until your name is entered as the registered proprietor on the proprietorship register by the Land Registry. This is deemed to happen as soon as your application for registration is received by the appropriate district land registry, which can be up to about three weeks after the property is transferred to you on completion. Thus, there is the added danger of a binding overriding interest arising (for example an informal right of way) in between the date of the actual transfer to you and the date of being registered as the new registered proprietor. The need, therefore, for a buyer to make careful enquiries and a close inspection of the property he is intending to buy cannot be overstressed.

So, question 7A on the form asked whether there were any rights of way, or right to lay a pipe, etc., and question 7B specifically deals with the rights of persons in actual occupation. Where there is someone else, beside the seller(s), living on the property, if that person also has an interest or rights in the property (by contributing towards the purchase price, for instance), that interest will bind a buyer as an overriding interest even after he has bought the property, unless when he asked that person what rights he had in the property, none were disclosed. The most likely persons to have such an interest are the seller's husband or wife (where only one spouse is the registered proprietor) or members of the seller's family, including their children. Mr and Mrs Timms were joint proprietors of 14 Twintree Avenue, so there was no question of either of them having an overriding interest. And Dodds & Son had confirmed in reply to 7B that no one other than they was living in the house.

If you discover that there is such a person living on the property you should insist that he (or she) be joined as a party to the contract, to show that he agrees to the sale; he cannot then assert any rights to the property later. Ideally, you should also insist that the person receives independent legal advice. This would put paid to any attempt by him to have the sale to you set aside by the court on the ground that he signed the contract while under the undue influence of the seller.

restrictions and planning

In reply to the question about restrictions, Matthew was told that as far as the seller knew, all the restrictive covenants had been complied with.

Question 9 was a multiple question dealing with planning. Paragraph A asked since when the property had had its present use, and whether that use was continuous. Basically, planning permission is needed for any material change of use. The reply confirmed that the property had been continuously used, since 1960, as a private dwellinghouse. 9B asked whether any building work or alterations had been carried out on the property in breach of planning control. The local authority can take enforcement proceedings (for example to pull down a garage); but when 4 years have elapsed from when the breach occurred (that is when the work was done) the local authority loses the right to take any further action. The four year rule does not apply to material changes of use except where the change is to use as a private dwellinghouse. The reply assured Matthew that no buildings had been erected nor alterations made to the house in the past four years. 9C requested the sellers to supply a copy of any planning permission for the present use and buildings. Dodds & Son had sent a copy of the original planning permission for 14 Twintree Avenue, and this confirmed their replies.

fixtures and fittings

Question 10 dealt with fixtures and fittings. Where an object is so attached to property as to become part of it, it is called a fixture and automatically passes to a buyer of the property unless specifically excluded from the sale. Examples of fixtures are extensions, fitted partitions, a boiler cemented to the floor. However, there are always some marginal items: light fittings, a greenhouse, television aerial, fitted cupboards, trees and roses, and so on, which might or might not be fixtures – if not, the seller is entitled to remove them. By asking the seller which of these items he intends to take with him, later disputes are, hopefully, avoided.

outgoings and completion

Question 11 asked for the rateable value of the property and whether any work had been carried out which might increase this.

The next question asked about completion and when vacant possession would be given. The answer was "7 March 1986" as Matthew and the Timms had agreed (but the date only becomes binding after exchange of contracts).

Question 12B referred to the Law Society's Code for Completion by post (1984 edition). This is a procedure for postal completion laid down by the Law Society which practising solicitors may follow if they wish. It only applies where both seller and buyer are represented by solicitors. A d-i-y buyer should not attempt a postal completion.

the supplementary enquiries

Matthew now turned to the replies Dodds & Son had given to his supplementary enquiries. They had written: 'Please rely on your own inspections and survey' against the first enquiry headed "Property". "Bit of a cop-out" said Matthew under his breath. Most solicitors prefer not to answer enquiries which deal with the fabric of a property, such as whether the property has structural defects, drainage defects, defective foundations. They fear misrepresenting the true state of affairs since these matters are more properly the province of a surveyor.

The second question dealt in more detail with "Services". Matthew learnt that the property had not been rewired since it was first built in 1960 and that was the last time the local electricity board had tested and approved the electricity system.

Sub-question (e) was inapplicable; there was mains drainage. The central heating system was presently in use and functioned to the Timms' satisfaction. There was no burglar alarm and no contracts for the maintenance and servicing of fixed appliances.

14 Twintree Avenue had no garage so the first sub-question on "vehicles" was inapplicable. Dodds & Son confirmed the road was not one in which parking was restricted.

The next question on 'Chattels and fixtures' informed him that the items mentioned in the estate agents' particulars were included in the sale. Matthew again made a note to remind Dodds & Son about the curtains and carpets. There were no hire-purchase or loan agreements that need concern him, and, yes, the telephone belonged to British Telecom.

In reply to the last enquiry, Dodds & Son told him the current amount payable in respect of the general and water rates and sewerage charge. The Timms were not buying another property, they were moving abroad, and they would make the appropriate arrangements for the meters to be read on 7 March.

Matthew was satisfied with the answers he had received to his preliminary enquiries. He was now ready to move on to the next stage, to approve the draft contract, subject to the question of the curtains and carpets being resolved.

approval of the draft contract

The custom between solicitors is that amendments to draft documents should appear in various colours, red first, then green and so on. However, in the case of contracts for the sale of residential property, many solicitors negotiate the terms of the contract by correspondence headed "subject to contract". Where alterations are minimal, as is probable in the case of a house with registered title absolute, the buyer should return the document unmarked (courtesy and tradition demand that he return the top copy), so that it can be used for signature by the seller without retyping, together with a covering letter stating that he approves the draft contract subject to his proposed amendment. If this amendment is approved by the seller's solicitor, the buyer can incorporate it in the copy of the contract he has retained, and use this for signature on his part.

Matthew therefore returned the top copy of the draft contract to Dodds & Son with the following covering letter:

38 Broadstone Drive
Hastings, Sussex

28 January 1986

To: Messrs Dodds & Son

Dear Sirs,

Re: 14 Twintree Avenue, Minford

Thank you for your letter of 24 January. I now return the draft contract which I approve, subject to satisfactory local searches and survey, and subject to some provision being made in it regarding the curtains and fitted carpets, which your clients agreed to include in the purchase price.

Assuming that your clients have no objection, and to save myself some stamp duty, I should prefer to pay for these separately on completion. This would involve amending the front page of the draft contract to read as follows:

Purchase money	£45,000.00
less deposit paid	4,500.00
	£40,500.00
Chattels, fittings etc	1,000.00
Balance	£41,500.00

and the addition of the special condition: "The buyer agrees to buy, and the sellers to sell, the curtains and fitted carpets at present on the property for the sum of £1,000 payable on completion".

Alternatively, if your clients wish the purchase price of the property to stand at £46,000, I suggest the addition of this special condition: "The curtains and fitted carpets at present on the property are included in the sale and purchase price".

When I have received back my local searches and heard from my surveyor and proposed mortgagees, I shall be ready to exchange contracts.

Yours faithfully,

M. J. Seaton

replies to local searches

At the beginning of the following week, Matthew received his local search certificate, and the replies to the enquiries he had made of Minford District Council on form 29A.

The local search certificate revealed that there was one registration affecting 14 Twintree Avenue at the date of the certificate. The 'attached schedule' described this entry as being that the property was in a smoke control area. This was quite normal for the area and presented no problems – the house had gas central heating.

The replies to the enquiries made on form Con.29A were also satisfactory. Minford District Council had supplied the answers on a standard printed sheet stapled to the form. These revealed that Twintree Avenue (there was no rear or other access road) was maintainable at the public expense, as were the sewer and drains serving the house; that there were no present proposals for road widening or for constructing any major roads in the area; that there were no repair, sanitary or other similar notices on the property; that the property was not likely to be compulsorily acquired or listed; and that the local plan for the district showed the area as zoned primarily for residential use. From the replies to his additional enquiries, he discovered that there were no proposals to stop up or divert Twintree Avenue, nor were there any pipelines in close proximity to the house.

Also, there were no enforcement proceedings being taken for breach of planning control.

enforcement

If there are enforcement proceedings, the answers to the local authority enquiries will show the number and date of the enforcement notice, and the planning regulation that has been breached, for example "Enforcement notice No.FN1234 dated 12 December 1985; breach of condition 4 on planning permission No.1764". The buyer should have been sent a copy of the notice with the replies to his preliminary enquiries, otherwise he should ask the seller or the seller's solicitor for one. Failing this he can ask the planning department of the local authority for the details of the notice.

Matthew heaved a sigh of relief. A colleague of his who was also doing her own conveyancing had recently discovered, from her enquiries of the district council, that there was an enforcement notice against the house she was hoping to buy. By inspecting the register of enforcement and stop notices kept by the district planning office, the colleague had discovered that her seller had built a garage a few months previously which did not conform to the specifications laid down in the planning permission. She was presently involved in negotiations with the other side for an assurance from the seller, by a special condition of sale to be included in the draft contract to the effect that the necessary work would be carried out to make the garage conform to the specifications before completion. Alternatively, she could have asked that the purchase price be reduced, so that she could have the work done after completion without being out of pocket.

beware

If you find anything in your searches which cannot be resolved by clarification by the local authority and/or subsequent negotiation with the other side, such as a proposal for compulsory acquisition, you should consult a solicitor or look for another property.

mortgage offer

That same day, Matthew received a letter from the Forthright Building Society:

FORTHRIGHT BUILDING SOCIETY

88 Lomax Street
Minford, Surrey

31 January 1986

To: M. J. Seaton Esq

Dear Sir,

Re: 14 Twintree Avenue, Minford

The Society has now received the report of its surveyor regarding the above property and is able to offer you an advance in the sum of £32,000 to be secured by a first legal charge (mortgage) on the above property. The loan is conditional upon completion taking place within three months of this date.

I enclose details of the proposed loan on our formal notification, from which you will see that the interest rate will be 12.75% per annum at first, but the society reserves the right to alter the interest rate on giving notice.

The loan will be repayable over a 25 year period by monthly instalments of £357.82 gross. The solicitors who will act for the society in connection with the legal formalities of the mortgage will be Messrs Hodgson, Green & Co of this town who will be getting in touch with you shortly.

Yours faithfully,

M. C. Templeton
Manager

For a mortgage loan of over £30,000, most building societies do not deduct the amount of tax relief and the borrower makes the monthly payments gross and will get the tax relief via his PAYE coding or his tax assessment (as used to happen with all mortgage loans before the introduction of MIRAS).

The enclosed notification and acceptance was in these terms:

Head Office:
Forthright House
Somerset Square
London EC3

Please reply to:
88 Lomax Street
Minford, Surrey

31 January 1986

To: Matthew J. Seaton Esq

Offer of advance

Re: 14 Twintree Avenue, Minford

Forthright Building Society offers to advance you the sum mentioned below, such sum to be secured on the above property, upon these terms and conditions:

1. The property is freehold/~~leasehold with years to run~~.
2. The offer is subject to the Society being finally satisfied as to your financial position and prospects.
3. Amount to be advanced £32,000 repayable by monthly repayments of £352.82 each over a period of 25 years. Each payment includes a proportion of principal and of interest.
4. Interest rate 12.75 per centum per annum. The right is reserved to vary this rate of interest on giving notice to do so. Effect may be given to variations of the interest rate by increasing or decreasing the period over which the payments are made (see para 3 above).
5. The property must throughout the period of the loan remain insured against fire and other risks in a sum equal to its reinstatement value (which may be higher than the market value); this at first is £55,000. The insurance will be arranged with a company approved by the Society.
6. The legal formalities in connection with the mortgage will be dealt with on behalf of the Society by the Society's solicitors Messrs Hodgson, Green & Co of 67 Lomax Street, Minford, Surrey. Their fees and disbursements are payable by you and are deducted from the loan when it is made. The loan is conditional upon the Society's solicitors being satisfied regarding the property's title and otherwise.
7. ~~The repairs listed in the accompanying schedule must~~ be ~~effected before completion/within months of completion~~.

8. The property must not be let in any way nor may alterations or additions be made to it without the Society's written consent, to be obtained in advance.
9. You have disclosed that *Emma Seaton* is or is intended to be an occupier of the property with you. The offer of advance has been issued on the basis that you have disclosed all such persons and that they will sign a declaration and request to be endorsed upon the mortgage as follows:
   'To the Society: Declaration and Request. I/We declare that I/we will assert no right to any overriding interest by occupation adverse to the Society's rights under the mortgage overleaf and I/we request you to make the advance accordingly.'
10. The Society reserves the right to modify or withdraw this offer at any time until the loan is effected.

G. Percy Marshall
Advance Manager

Not all building societies necessarily send a letter with their mortgage offer; some incorporate appropriate wording into the preamble to the offer of advance (thereby avoiding unnecessary correspondence). Details of the society's solicitor would then be given on the offer of advance. Some building societies enclose their *Rules for borrowers* which will be incorporated in the mortgage document. Some supply the applicant with more information than the Forthright did; this may be presented in a mortgage folder which includes general conditions regarding the mortgage advance, method of calculation, insurance details.

Clause 2 of the Forthright's offer would not appear where a building society decides on the applicant's financial position before ever making a mortgage offer.

Building societies and banks and other lenders nearly always include a requirement like Forthright Building Society's point 9 in their offers of advance. This is a result of a decision by the House of Lords which suggests that a wife, co-habitor, parent or other person living in the property may have rights, or have acquired rights, in the property which are capable of binding a mortgagee as an overriding interest even though the property is not in that person's name. Mortgagees therefore ask that all people likely to be living on the property should sign an undertaking, either as a separate document or an endorsement on the mortgage, that they will not exert their right (if any) to stay on in the house if the owner should fail to repay the loan and the Society has to sell the property to recover its debt. Matthew's wife Emma would have to sign a 'Declaration and request' (sometimes the undertaking is called a deed of consent or postponement or release).

In another recent case, a wife successfully argued that she had not consented to a mortgage of her home (which was owned by her husband) by signing a deed of release: she signed the deed under the undue influence of her husband and it was therefore invalid. For this reason, your building society or other lender may insist that anyone you intend to live with you should sign the undertaking in the presence of an independent solicitor.

It is normal for the borrower to have to pay the legal costs of the building society's solicitors, usually in the form of a deduction from the mortgage loan. Similarly, where the loan is from a bank, the bank generally instructs an authorised solicitor to examine, and prepare a report on, the title to the property and to deal with the completion formalities on behalf of the bank. Where the buyer is a customer of the bank, he may be informed that the amount of the solicitor's fees will be debited to his account, rather than deducted from the loan.

In Matthew's case, it was possible that Hodgson, Green & Co acted generally for the Minford branch of the building society. Some building societies, particularly the larger ones, adopt a panel system, whereby many solicitors all over the country are on a panel of solicitors who can act for them. In this way it often happens that the same solicitor acts for the buyer and for the building society, with a saving in legal fees to the buyer as a result.

it is only an offer

It is quite normal to find that a loan has to be taken up within a set number of months, otherwise the offer to lend the money lapses. With some building societies, the offer can be withdrawn if it is not accepted within a specified time (such as one month) or the mortgage is not completed within, say, three months from the date of the offer. In practice, a building society is often willing to extend the time limit if the delay is explained.

There was nothing binding, either on the building society or on Matthew about the offer of a mortgage: Clause 10 of the official notification made this clear. Theoretically at least, the buyer of a house may be placed in a vulnerable position. He has to commit himself to the seller by a binding contract on the strength of an offer from a building society, which is not binding, to lend him part of the purchase price. If for some reason, such as the lender finding that the buyer's financial circumstances have taken a serious turn for the worse, the building society were to back out before the loan was made, the buyer could do nothing about it. Generally, the freedom to withdraw the offer is only invoked in fairly dire circumstances. However, the proposed interest rate may be increased after the building society's formal offer.

The form from the Forthright Building Society was in duplicate, an original and tear-off copy. A notice on the back of the form warned that 'in the event of Forthright Building Society making you an advance to assist you in the purchase of the property the making of the advance will not imply any warranty by the Society that the purchase price is reasonable.' This was a formality required under the Building Societies Act 1962, which the society put in to cover itself on this question.

There was also reference to MIRAS (mortgage interest relief at source) by which basic rate taxpayers make their repayments net of tax rather than tax relief being allowed via PAYE coding or their assessment at the end of the tax year.

MIRAS, while normal, is not an automatic right. The prospective borrower must feel able to complete form MIRAS 70; the lender must equally feel satisfied that the transaction is eligible and that all the money will be used for a purpose covered by the MIRAS regulations. Where any doubt exists on either side, form MIRAS 3 must be completed by the applicant and sent to his own Inland Revenue authority who will decide and then notify a decision to both lender and applicant.

The terms of the offer were as Matthew had expected. He felt able to sign and return the Forthright's form of acceptance at the bottom of the copy of the mortgage offer.

ACCEPTANCE

3 February 1986

To:
Forthright Building Society

I, *Matthew J. Seaton of 38 Broadstone Drive, Hastings, Sussex* accept your offer to make an advance to be secured on 14 Twintree Avenue, Minford, Surrey, upon the terms and conditions made known to me.

~~My solicitors are~~

Signed
M. J. Seaton

The offer of advance may be a multi-set form, one of the sheets of which has an acceptance of the terms and conditions of the offer which the borrower signs and returns.

Matthew had not yet heard from Andrew Robertson & Co with their report on the survey they had carried out for him. He knew from the society's letter of 31 January that they had inspected the property. He telephoned Mr James Robertson, who told him that his report was in draft and he would be receiving it shortly.

the amended draft contract

The third piece of correspondence Matthew received that day was a letter from Dodds & Son:

DODDS & SON
Solicitors

1 Charter Street
Minford, Surrey

31 January 1986

To: M. J. Seaton Esq

Dear Sir,

Re: 14 Twintree Avenue, Minford

We thank you for your letter of 28 January, returning the draft contract. We regret to inform you that our clients are not willing to reduce the purchase price of the property below £46,000, although they remain happy to include the curtains and carpets in that price. Accordingly we have included your alternative suggested amendment as Clause H in the special conditions of sale: "The curtains and fitted carpets at present on the property are included in the sale and purchase price". We are treating the top copy as an engrossment of the contract.

We are obtaining our clients' signatures to the contract and on receipt of the part signed by you and the deposit, we shall let you have the part signed by the sellers and the balance of the title.

Yours faithfully,
DODDS & SON

Matthew felt that the Timms were being a little unreasonable in not allowing the price of the curtains and carpets to be stated separately in the contract. Still, this would only have saved him £10 in stamp duty and decided to accept matters as they were.

When the wording of a contract is agreed, each side prepares a fair copy of it which is called an engrossment. If the contract is approved as originally drafted, or with only minor variations, each side uses their copy of the draft contract as the engrossment itself. The seller then signs the engrossed contract held by his solicitor and the buyer signs the one held by him or his solicitor.

As will happen in Matthew's case a little later on, the contract is made by the parties swopping their signed contracts.

Matthew would ask his secretary at the office if she would kindly type the new clause H in the copy of the draft contract form he had retained, so that he could use it as his engrossment.

insurance

One further matter a buyer should attend to before exchange of contracts: insurance of the house.

Once contracts are exchanged, the risk in the property passes to the buyer and, generally speaking, the seller is under no duty to maintain any insurance on it. Both sets of conditions of sale state this clearly: Law Society general condition 11, and National condition 21. Thus if, for example, the property is flooded between exchange of contracts and completion, the buyer would still have to go through with the purchase and bear the cost of repairs. So, the insurance of the property you are buying should start from the moment you exchange contracts.

A buyer should insure the property for risks such as fire, storm, flood, damage by burglars and to cover the owner's liability for accidents to third parties caused by the state of the property – a roof tile falling down and injuring someone, for instance. A building policy covers these risks. Eventually, Matthew would need a policy that covers contents as well as building.

taking over the seller's insurance?

It may be possible to take over the seller's existing policy, but the more common practice today (except in the case of a leasehold house, when it may be better to take over a policy which complies with the lease) is to take out a new one.

If you are taking over an existing policy, the reply to question IV on the *Enquiries before contract* form (for leasehold properties) should give you details of the policy. You can then write to the insurance company and advise them of your interest in the property. On completion, you would have to pay back to the seller a proportionate part of the premium he has paid. After completion, the policy would have to be sent to the insurance company so that your interest and that of your mortgagee (if any) can be formally noted on the policy and in their records. If you wish, you can, of course, adjust the amount of cover.

It is, however, usually much better to take out a new policy, making sure that the property is neither over-insured nor under-insured. If you already have an insurance company with which you are satisfied, get a proposal form for a household building policy and ask for cover to start immediately contracts have been exchanged; then inform your company when this has happened and pay the first premium.

insurance when there is a mortgage

If, as in Matthew's case, you are obtaining a loan from a building society, the society will almost certainly suggest that you insure through an insurance company it knows well. The mortgage application form may contain an application for insurance.

A building society obviously has a strong vested interest in the insurance; if the property were to burn down, uninsured, most of their security would have gone up in smoke. The insurance policy will have a note of their mortgage endorsed on it.

On Matthew's application form from the Forthright Building Society, there had been a section about insurance. Normally a borrower is entitled to choose from a number of named insurance companies. If he wants to use another company (perhaps his current insurers) he would have to get the lender's approval. The manager of the society had suggested the Bridstow Insurance Company Ltd which had a local office nearby, and Matthew had agreed. Matthew did not have to fill in a proposal form himself, the matter was completely handled by the society.

Where a building society insures its borrowers' property through a special block policy with the insurance company, the borrower will not get a copy of the insurance policy. He should, however, make sure that he gets all the relevant details from the society. An advantage of a building society's block policy may be that the borrower can have an ally if a claim were to be refused by an insurance company for some obscure reason. The sheer volume of business generated by the society to that particular company would enable pressure to be brought to bear if the borrower was able to satisfy his building society that he had been unfairly treated.

Some, but not all, building societies pay the first premium to make sure that the insurance is effective, and deduct the amount from the loan to the buyer. Similarly, some building societies also pay the subsequent insurance premiums and add the amount each year to one of the monthly mortgage payments, or allow the borrower to pay part of the premium each month. The Forthright would notify Matthew how much his premium was.

There is one point to bear in mind. Generally a building society will insure a building from exchange of contracts. But where it insures a property from the date a mortgage advance is released (at completion), there may be an uninsured gap of a few weeks, because a purchaser becomes liable for any damage caused to the property from exchange of contracts.

Whether you yourself take out the insurance or the building society does, check that the sum insured is adequate to cover the cost of wholly rebuilding the property, after allowing for architects' and surveyors' fees and the cost of clearing the site of debris, in the case of total destruction.

There can be quite a difference between the market value of a house and its reinstatement value. Where the reinstatement value is higher than the market value, it is on this amount that a building society takes out insurance, not on the amount of the market value or amount of the mortgage loan.

contents insurance

Whether you are buying with the aid of a mortgage or not, you should make sure that contents insurance starts as soon as there is any of your own property inside the house. If the seller agrees to leave certain items in the house, contents insurance may have to be taken out on exchange of contracts, depending on which contract form is used. If the sale is governed by the National conditions of sale, the risk in the items probably passes to the buyer on exchange of contracts, so they should (if valuable) be insured by him from that date. But under Law Society general condition 24 the items remain the seller's responsibility until completion.

It is sensible to take out a contents policy with the same company as the building is insured with. It is quite likely that the building society will want to help you arrange contents as well as buildings insurance. Some now offer a combined buildings and contents policy.

the building society's solicitors

After the weekend, Matthew heard from the solicitors acting for the Forthright Building Society:

HODGSON, GREEN & CO
Solicitors

67 Lomax Street
Minford, Surrey

3 February 1986

To: Matthew J. Seaton Esq

Dear Sir,

Re: 14 Twintree Avenue, Minford

Our clients Forthright Building Society have instructed us with regard to an advance on mortgage of £32,000 to be made to you and to be secured on the above property. We understand that you will be acting for yourself in this matter.

When the legal formalities regarding your purchase are sufficiently advanced, please let us have the following documents: contract, preliminary enquiries and replies, local searches, office copies of the entries on the Register and filed plan, authority for us to inspect the Register, requisitions on title and replies and draft transfer as approved by the vendors' solicitors.

Yours faithfully,
HODGSON, GREEN & CO

This was a normal introductory letter and, apart from a routine acknowledgment, no further action was needed with Hodgson, Green & Co until after exchange of contracts. If there had been anything that might worry the building society's solicitors (for instance, a possible breach of covenant or evidence of a boundary dispute), Matthew should have written immediately to Hodgson,

Green & Co, and not waited until after exchange of contracts. Otherwise there would have been a risk of the building society withdrawing their mortgage offer after Matthew had already committed himself to the purchase by exchanging contracts.

In fact, where there is any doubt about the mortgage loan from the building society or other lender, the buyer should not commit himself until he is sure that he will get the money. Some solicitors would advise that, instead of Matthew's routine acknowledgment of the letter from the building society's solicitors at this stage a buyer should send to them the first of the documents they will require (draft contract, preliminary enquiries and replies, local searches, office copies of entries on the register, filed plan) before he proceeds to the stage of exchanging contracts. This would mean delaying things if he is waiting for replies to his search and enquiries from the local authority, but the building society's solicitors would do their own search (as many do, anyway).

personal inspections

Matthew knew that he would probably be in a position to exchange contracts within the next few days. It was high time for him to make certain personal inspections. These, together with his surveyor's report, would complete his pre-contract investigations. He would take the afternoon off from work and spend it in Surrey, visiting the local authority and the house. He phoned the Timms to make sure that this was convenient.

The local land charges search and enquiries had given Matthew information of a public nature directly relevant to 14 Twintree Avenue. He and Emma planned to make Minford their home for many years, so he wanted to know more about the probable future development of Minford and the surrounding area.

A leaflet prepared by the Royal Town Planning institute to help people make better use of the planning system includes some paragraphs on **how do I find out for myself?**

> "If you want to find out more, you should go to the planning department of the council who collect the rates for the property.

> This will be the district or borough council [in England or Wales].
> If you ask to see someone in the planning department you should be given all the help you need. It is a good idea to ring first so that you can make an appointment, give time for all the relevant information to be put together and have a trip around the area yourself on the lookout for anything you may want to ask about. Make sure that the person you see knows that you want to buy the property and need to know beforehand if there is a restriction on it or things might be happening nearby which could affect the building or its surroundings. The planning staff will be helpful, but remember one thing in particular, if you buy a house because of the view, there is no guarantee that it will stay that way. Other people may want to build across it and town planning, although it takes into account privacy, overlooking and overshadowing, cannot protect your view over someone else's land."

Matthew went first to Guildford to look at the structure plan for the whole area which was kept at Surrey County Council planning offices. This contained the county council's long term plans for the area regarding such matters as housing, transportation and industrial development. Then he went on to see the local plan kept by Minford District Council planning authority, which applied these long-term plans to the specific district of Minford, and would, for example, show the site for a new school or the proposed route of a new trunk road to ease traffic flow.

Matthew found the people at both planning offices extremely helpful and willing to explain the meaning of the plans to him. As far as he could judge, nothing that was planned was likely to affect 14 Twintree Avenue adversely. But he bore in mind the warning he had been given at both offices that these plans could change in the future.

planning permission matters

While he was at the district council planning offices, he asked to see the register of planning applications and decisions. This showed that planning permission had been given to Minford Estate Developments Ltd in 1958 to build the estate of houses which now included 14 Twintree Avenue. By looking at the plans for the estate which the council had approved, Matthew was able to identify 14 Twintree Avenue and to check that the house built was the same as that for which permission had been given. The register also confirmed that no major development had been approved for any neighbouring property. Finally Matthew was pleased to see that if he decided to build a garage on the property planning permission was likely to be granted. Several such permissions had already been granted to the owners of other houses in the street.

The replies to a buyer's local searches may also make it necessary for him to ask to see the register of enforcement and stop notices or the register of listed buildings. If there has been a breach of planning control, the former will tell him what steps are necessary to remedy the breach and by what date; the latter register will tell him what extra planning controls exist in relation to the property, such as specifications regarding external decoration and repair.

Matthew came away from the local authority offices with a much better idea about the locality, present and future.

looking at the house

It is always advisable to compare the description of the property in the contract and the plan with the actual property to make sure that they correspond. If they do not, you should raise the question with the seller and, if necessary, consult a solicitor. And, because of the *caveat emptor* rule, it is important for a buyer to make a thorough inspection of the property before exchanging contracts.

Matthew had arranged with the Timms to visit the house at 4 o'clock in the afternoon and he arrived with a few minutes to spare. He had with him the copy of the filed plan Dodds & Son had sent him and compared the plan with the actual property to see whether the plan was correct. It was, and he noted in passing that no alterations or extensions had been made to the house which might have required planning permission. He also saw that there was nothing on the property which could be the cause of confusion or disputes with neighbours in the future, such as a row of trees near the boundary of a garden. And yes, the property was connected to the mains services and everything appeared to be working properly.

extra occupants?

Matthew was especially careful to check that there was no one other than Mr and Mrs Timms in the house, or signs of any other occupants in the house or outside in the garden. If he had found someone there, he would have asked their reason for being on the property and if necessary whether they had any stake or rights in it. If they had, he would have asked Dodds & Son to obtain their signature to the contract.

cracks or defects?

The buyer of a house, new, second-hand, or converted, with the benefit of a current National House Building guarantee should pay particular attention to any cracks or other signs of defects in the house. Remember that the NHBC scheme only works if prompt notice in writing of any defects is given either to the builder or the council. The physical condition of the property is also of particular importance to the buyer of a leasehold house. He must ensure that it complies with the repairing obligations under the lease because both Law Society general condition 8(5) and National condition 11(7) exclude any warranty on the seller's part that these have been performed.

the surveyor's report

Matthew's surveyor's report arrived the following morning. Basically it told him that the house was structurally sound, but had some petty faults which were largely design errors and could not now be rectified. There were a couple of loose tiles on the roof and some cracks would need making good. Apart from this, the house was in good order. There was nothing in the surveyor's report to deter Matthew from buying the house or to justify his asking for a reduction in the purchase price.

He decided it was time to think about contents insurance although he did not intend to insure the contents until his own furniture and belongings were moved in and would take a chance on the curtains and carpets the Timms were leaving behind. He wrote to the Bridstow Insurance Co, requesting a proposal form for contents insurance on the house.

exchange of contracts

By far the most common way of bringing a contract for the sale and purchase of a house into existence is by 'exchange of contracts'. This method of making the contract legally binding is contemplated by both the Law Society and the National conditions. The contract really consists of two identical documents and an 'exchange of contracts' is when one party (or his solicitor), having received the other party's signed contract, posts his signed contract to the other party (or his solicitor).

By tradition, it is the buyer who sends his contract first. If your purchase is not dependent on the sale of your present, or some other, property, you can send off your signed contract as soon as you have completed your searches and enquiries, received your survey report and mortgage offer and inspected the property.

The procedure is that you send off your signed contract with a cheque for the deposit (less any preliminary deposit you may have paid to the estate agent). When it is received by the seller's solicitor, he will date both parts, insert the completion date into both parts (unless this has already been done) and send the seller's signed contract back to you. Contracts are now exchanged. In cases of dispute, contracts are deemed to be exchanged when the seller's solicitor commits the seller's signed contract to the post (Law Society general condition 10(1), National condition 1(7)(ii)). Remember that if the contract incorporates the Law Society's general conditions, you will need a banker's draft for the deposit (condition 9(1)).

Occasionally, if both sides live in the same town, exchange of contracts is done in person, usually at the seller's solicitor's office. The buyer (or his solicitor) hands over his signed part and the deposit and in return the seller (or his solicitor) hands over the seller's signed part. The date of the contract is the date of the meeting. An advantage of exchanging contracts in person would be that the buyer then knows exactly when the contract is made (and he could withdraw it up to that moment) whereas in postal exchange he will not know exactly when the seller's solicitor has sent off the contract so that he has become bound.

exchange by telephone

Problems of timing involved in chain transactions have led to a new practice among solicitors of 'exchange of contracts by telephone' and the Law Society has issued guidelines to its members as to the procedure to be adopted. However, even between solicitors the practice is fraught with difficulties and only used where there is no other viable method of exchanging contracts at short notice. It is not recommended that a buyer acting without a solicitor attempt a telephone exchange.

if there is a chain

If your purchase is dependent on the sale of your present or other property, it is obvious that you should receive your buyer's signed purchase contract and his deposit before you send your signed contract and deposit to your seller's solicitor.

problems with the deposit

A buyer may have difficulty in finding the ready cash to pay the 10 per cent deposit, especially if he is using the money from selling his present home for buying the new one. Do not ignore the possibility of asking the seller to accept a deposit of less than 10 per cent.

If the deposit is still problematical, a bank's bridging (or bridgover) loan can prove useful, although fairly expensive (about 3 or 4 per cent above base rate, plus an 'arrangement fee'). A bank will generally make a bridging loan to a buyer for the amount of the deposit only after contracts for the sale of his present home (or other property) have actually been exchanged. However, some banks are quite prepared to consider 'open' as well as 'closed' bridgovers; each case is taken on its merits. If the amount involved is not large in relation to the property values they may assist with an 'open' bridgover. The potential dangers regarding the possible delays would be highlighted to the customer, as well as the likely cost of interest – which could be considerable.

A bank will normally require an undertaking from the buyer's solicitor that when he receives the sale money (from the property his client is selling), he will retain sufficient to repay the bridging loan for the deposit for the house his client is buying. If you are doing your own conveyancing, the solicitor of the buyer of your present home or other property may consent to giving such an undertaking to your bank, on payment of a small fee – but the Law Society considers such an undertaking ill-advised. Or a deposit could be passed from your buyer's solicitor to the solicitor of the person from whom you are buying, thus 'leap-frogging' you and avoiding the problem of a solicitor not being willing to hand a deposit to a non-solicitor.

Although a bridging loan for the deposit can sometimes be arranged with the help of a bank or the building society's or your own buyer's solicitors, it would seem that for a first time buyer doing his own conveyancing, who has a 95 or 100 per cent mortgage, there is likely to be considerable difficulty in obtaining institutional finance additional to his mortgage. So if you are a first time buyer with the aid of a 95 or 100 per cent mortgage from a building society and you need bridging finance to pay the deposit, there is a risk that your efforts to do your own conveyancing may have to end.

Matthew's exchange

A buyer should not consider himself ready to exchange contracts until

- the form and wording of the contract has been agreed
- he has received satisfactory replies to his preliminary enquiries
- the local land charges search certificate and replies to enquiries made of the local authority are satisfactory
- he has made arrangements to borrow on mortgage the amount he needs and has not had any adverse news from the mortgagees or their solicitors
- he has received a satisfactory report from a surveyor
- he has made a satisfactory inspection of the property
- arrangements have been made for the property to be insured
- he has the necessary finance for the deposit.

Matthew had spoken to the Forthright Building Society to check if there were any problems about his mortgage. He was now ready to send to Dodds & Son his signed contract to buy 14 Twintree Avenue and a cheque for the deposit (he had arranged with his bank to collect a draft on thursday morning).

He sent his signed contract to Dodds & Son by first class post with this letter:

38 Broadstone Drive
Hastings, Sussex

6 February 1986

To: Messrs Dodds & Son

Dear Sirs,

Re: 14 Twintree Avenue, Minford

I now enclose the contract signed by me and a banker's draft for £4,600 in respect of the deposit.

I look forward to receiving from you as soon as possible the contract signed by your clients and dated, and separate authorities to inspect the register in favour of myself and Messrs Hodgson, Green & Co, who are the solicitors acting for my mortgagees, the Forthright Building Society.

Yours faithfully,
M. J. Seaton

contents insurance

Matthew heard from the Bridstow Insurance Co Ltd sending him a proposal form for house contents insurance. He would need to give this some thought and put a realistic value on his belongings. He decided to complete the form during the weekend.

Soon afterwards Matthew heard from Dodds & Son:

DODDS & SON
Solicitors

1 Charter Street
Minford, Surrey

7 February 1986

To: M. J. Seaton Esq

Dear Sir,

Re: 14 Twintree Avenue, Minford

We thank you for your letter of yesterday's date enclosing contract duly signed and banker's draft for £4,600 in our favour being the deposit, receipt of which we hereby acknowledge.

We now have pleasure in enclosing by way of exchange contract signed by our clients, Mr and Mrs Timms. We have dated both parts of the contract with today's date and have inserted completion date of 7 March 1986.

We further enclose an authority to inspect the Register in favour of yourself and an additional one in favour of Messrs Hodgson, Green & Co, as requested.

We await your requisitions on title and draft transfer for approval in due course.

Yours faithfully,
DODDS & SON

As contracts had now been exchanged and had become legally binding on both sides, Matthew telephoned the Forthright Building Society to ask them to effect immediate insurance cover for the house and sent a confirmatory letter.

STAGE II – CONTRACT TO COMPLETION

Before exchange of contracts, the buyer's task is mainly to check various things about the property; his post-contract work consists of investigating the seller's title, getting the ownership of the property transferred to him, obtaining his mortgage finance and paying the purchase price to the seller. In the case of property registered with title absolute, the Land Registry takes care of most of the post-contract work, leaving just a few formalities to be attended to.

the seller's title

After exchange of contracts, the seller's solicitor must prove the seller's ownership of the property and that it can be properly transferred to the buyer. He does this by supplying the buyer (or his solicitor) with

- office copies of the entries on the register
- the filed plan and any documents noted on the register in so far as they are relevant to the property
- copies of documents creating or evidence of any rights affecting the property as to which the register is inconclusive or which are not required to be registered (if he has not already done so), and
- an authority to inspect the register.

Most seller's solicitors send a full set of office copies and any other copy documents to the buyer with the draft contract (a practice encouraged by the Law Society), so that all you will receive after the contract is made is an authority to inspect the register.

Office copies bear the date on which they were issued by the Land Registry, and show what is on the register at that date. A buyer must make sure that there has been no change in the register between the date of the issue of the office copies and the date on which he completes his purchase. To do this, he will make another search of the register, called an official search, a short time before completion. The certificate of official search received back from the Land Registry would reveal any such change.

The register is not open to public inspection. Hence the need for authority to inspect the register, that is the seller's written permission for the buyer to inspect the register, which the buyer must send to the Land Registry with his application for an official search.

A buyer's mortgagee is also concerned with the state of the seller's title and he needs to make an official search of the register before the mortgage is completed for the same reasons as the buyer. This is why Matthew had asked Dodds & Son for an additional authority for Hodgson, Green & Co (his mortgagees's solicitors) to inspect the register.

Matthew had already studied carefully the office copies of the entries on the register and the filed plan of 14 Twintree Avenue which Dodds & Son had sent him with the draft contract. He was satisfied that the description of the property in the property register and the filed plan corresponded with that which he was buying and that Mr and Mrs Timms were the joint registered proprietors with title absolute. Provided that both were parties to and executed the deed of transfer, he was assured of getting good title to the property. Matthew had also noted the implications of the restrictive covenants in favour of Minford Estate Developments entered on the charges register, and that the house was subject to an existing mortgage in favour of Minford Building Society which would have to be discharged on completion. Had he come across any other restriction, caution, inhibition or notice in his office copies he would have followed the procedure outlined earlier at pages 52 to 57.

On the whole, the likelihood of an adverse entry (other than a restriction in the case of joint proprietors, restrictive covenants or a registered charge for a mortgage) appearing on a normal house-seller's title is rare. If, however, you find an entry which you are not quite sure about, every district land registry has an excellent enquiry department that will answer reasonable enquiries about registered property not only from solicitors but also members of the public. Furthermore, each district land registry has a number of qualified legal employees on the staff who can be consulted if necessary. So if you should be faced with such a problem, telephone or visit the experts.

requisitions on title: buyer to seller

After the buyer (or his solicitor) has completed his examination of the seller's title, he will compile and send to the seller's solicitor a list of additional questions about the property called 'requisitions on title'. Most solicitors make standard enquiries on a printed form of requisitions, form Conveyancing 28B *Requisitions on Title* (the current version is of February 1984). The form incorporates, by reference, the preliminary enquiries made before exchange of contracts (any change in the replies to these are required to be detailed by question 1) thus shortening the list of enquiries that have to be made. (In the rare case of no preliminary enquiries having been made, a 'long' version of Conveyancing 28B is available from Oyez).

Certain questions on the form should be deleted if they are irrelevant, such as those that relate to leaseholds when you are buying a freehold. Matthew crossed out 2(B) (dealing with rent and insurance) and question 6 (dealing with notification about the sale of the property) because these are only relevant to leasehold or tenanted property. He also crossed out question 3. 3(A) applies to unregistered land and although 3(B) does apply to registered land, it need only be asked (i) where the buyer has merely been supplied with a photocopy of the seller's land or charge certificate, (ii) where he is buying a plot on a registered building estate, or (iii) where he is buying part only of registered land, in which case the seller's land certificate may be on deposit at the Land Registry. In any of these circumstances, the buyer needs the information requested in question 3(B) to make his official search of the register. 7(B) and (C) were inappropriate too.

They concern the immediate or telegraphic transfer of funds where completion is to be by post.

Question 2(A) asked for receipts for rates and other outgoings to be produced and arrears allowed for and 2(C) asked for a completion statement, which tells the buyer exactly what he will have to pay on completion.

Question 4 referred to subsisting mortgages and required that proof would have to be given that the Timms' mortgage had been paid off and asked how this would be done. Where property is subject to a registered charge (as was 14 Twintree Avenue at present and as are most registered houses where there is a mortgage) the building society uses a Land Registry form (form 53) to discharge the charge (mortgage). The Land Registry then cancels the entries on the register relating to the charge. But for some strange reason building societies (and other lenders) often find it difficult for form 53 to be ready on completion and, instead, the seller's solicitor hands over an undertaking to provide it within so-many days. The question asks whether form 53 would be used on completion or an undertaking, and if the latter, what it would say.

Question 5(A)(i) states that vacant possession must be given on completion. 5(A)(ii) which asks: "Has every person in occupation of all or any part of the property agreed to vacate on or before completion?", concerns the problem of an occupational overriding interest. The aim of the question is to ensure that the buyer will not be saddled with the interests or claims of such persons. Where the sale is governed by the National conditions of sale, the reply will help the buyer decide whether to insist on his right, under condition 5(4), to go into possession of the property on or immediately before completion, so that when the property is transferred to him he is the only one on the property. There is no equivalent provision in the Law Society general conditions.

Question 5(A)(iii) then asks what arrangements are to be made about handing over keys. 5(B) being applicable only to property subject to an existing tenancy, Matthew crossed it out.

Finally question 7(A) asked where completion would take place and about payment.

There is extra space on the form for making additional requisitions. (It would be rare for anything to be filled in here, in an ordinary domestic conveyance.)

time limits

Both the National and Law Society conditions of sale impose time limits on the making of requisitions, and for this purpose time is of the essence. This means that the buyer has to deliver his requisitions to the seller within a specified time, otherwise the seller can refuse to answer them (in practice this is unusual), and the buyer has to accept the seller's title. Under Law Society general condition 15(2) the requisitions must be made within 6 working days of the receipt of the complete seller's title (that is office copies, copy documents, authority to inspect the register and other information statutorily required to be supplied), or the date of the contract whichever is the later. National condition 9(3) gives him 11 working days from the date of receipt of all the seller's title. Under the Law Society general conditions the seller's solicitor has to reply within four working days, but under the National conditions he has merely to reply within a reasonable time of receiving the requisitions.

Matthew signed and dated the form of requisitions on title and sent it to Dodds & Son, together with an extra copy for their file. The extra copy was a matter of politeness so that they would have a record of the questions and the answers they give.

the transfer

Next, Matthew prepared the draft transfer. This document, when signed, sealed and delivered, is effectual between the parties to transfer the ownership of the house to the buyer. He does not however become the legal owner of the house until the transfer is registered by the Land Registry. Because of the time it takes the Land Registry to register dealings, this is deemed to be the date on which the buyer's application for registration is received at the appropriate district land registry.

The transfer form is easy to fill in. Where the transfer is of the whole of registered property (that is, where the title number covers just the one property and it is that property which is being sold and bought) you should use form 19 TRANSFER OF WHOLE. If you are buying the property in the joint names of yourself and your husband or wife, or some other person, use form 19(JP). Where only part of the registered property is being transferred (say one house out of ten) form 20 should be used. The forms are applicable to freehold or leasehold property.

On page 110 is what the front page of Matthew's draft transfer looked like.

The space at the top of the form was left blank for the time being. After completion, the Inland Revenue would emboss the appropriate stamps when the transfer had been produced to them and the stamp duty paid. Also left blank for the time being were the date (hopefully 7 March would appear here).

Matthew used the office copy of the entries on the register to complete the form. The property register gave him the name of the county and district, a short description of the property and the title number. The proprietorship register supplied him with the Timms' full names and occupations.

Mr and Mrs Timms were selling as trustees for sale; Matthew therefore crossed out the words "beneficial owners". If the contract in your case states that the seller is selling in a capacity other than beneficial owner, for example personal representative or, as in the Timms' case, trustee for sale, the words "beneficial owner" should be crossed out and the appropriate title inserted. Remember that if your seller is a tenant for life or trustee for sale, you will require a receipt from at least two trustees (the trustees of the settlement in the case of settled land). This is achieved by making them parties to the transfer so that they both 'sign, seal and deliver' the transfer.

co-ownership

The form to use if you are buying a property jointly (whether as tenants in common or as joint tenants) is form 19(JP). The front of the form is the same as form 19, but the back contains the

Form 19

H.M. Land Registry — Land Registration Acts, 1925 to 1971

Stamp pursuant to section 28 of the Finance Act, 1931, to be impressed here	*When the transfer attracts Inland Revenue duty, the stamps should be impressed here before lodging the transfer for registration*

(1) TRANSFER OF WHOLE

(Rule 98 or 115, Land Registration Rules 1925)

County and district (or London borough) Surrey, Minford

Title number(s) SY 4327 1604

Property 14 Twintree Avenue, Minford

Date .... 1986 ... In consideration of

fortysix thousand pounds

pounds (£46,000 —) (2) *the receipt whereof is hereby acknowledged*

I/We(3) William Herbert Timms, engineer and Margaret Edna Timms, housewife, both of 14 Twintree Avenue, Minford, Surrey

(4) *as ~~beneficial~~ owner(s)* trustees for sale hereby transfer to:

(5) MATTHEW JOHN SEATON of 38 BROADSTONE DRIVE HASTINGS SUSSEX, ACCOUNTANT

(6) (Company registration number ....)

the land comprised in the title(s) above mentioned (7) (8)

(1) *For a transfer by a company or corporation form 19(Co) is printed and for a transfer to joint proprietors form 19(JP) is printed.*

(2) *Strike out if not required.*

(3) *In BLOCK LETTERS, enter full name(s), postal address(es) and occupation(s) of the proprietor(s) of the land.*

(4) *If desired or otherwise as the case may be (see rule 76 and 77).*

(5) *In BLOCK LETTERS, enter full name, postal address and occupation of the transferee for entry on the register.*

(6) *On a transfer to a Company registered under the Companies Acts, insert here the Company's registration number if entry thereof on the register is desired.*

(7) *Any special clause should be entered here.*

(8) *A transfer for charitable uses should follow form 36 in the schedule to the Land Registration Rules, 1925 (see rules 121 and 122).*

(continued overleaf)

following declaration: "The transferees declare that the survivor of them can/cannot give a valid receipt for capital money arising on a disposition of the land." Cross out "cannot" if you have agreed to hold the house as joint tenants, and "can" if you have agreed to be tenants in common.

A further difference on form 19(JP) is that there are extra attestation clauses (places for signature etc). Both buyers will have to sign the eventual transfer (and then the seller) because they have agreed to do something (that is, hold as joint tenants or tenants in common) within the body of the transfer. They do not need to have a different witness each, but one co-owner should not sign as witness to the other's signature.

getting the transfer ready

On both forms 19 and 19(JP) there is a space at the bottom of the front page for any special clauses that may have to be added, should this be necessary. Sometimes a seller's solicitor will want a clause in the transfer to the effect that the buyer will comply with certain restrictive and/or positive covenants (for example to maintain a private road) and will indemnify the seller for any future liability that might arise from a breach of the covenants. The contract will tell you (in the special conditions of sale) if such a clause is required and the precise form it should take, so you can copy it from the contract into the transfer form; if you do not, the seller's solicitor will probably add it when approving the draft transfer. There is no reason why a buyer should not accept such a clause. It does, however, mean that the buyer has to execute the transfer as well as the seller, because he is agreeing to do something, in the body of the deed.

certificate of value

At the end of form 19 and form 19(JP) before the attestation clause, is a certificate of value. Note 9 requests the user to delete the certificate if it is not required.

The only time it will be required is if the purchase price of the property is £30,000 or less, to take advantage of the nil rate of stamp duty. If you are paying £30,000 or less for your house, then insert the figure £30,000 (not the actual purchase price) at the end of the certificate of value. Matthew deleted the certificate. He was paying £46,000 for 14 Twintree Avenue and would have to pay £460 stamp duty (that is, 1 per cent of the purchase price).

Lawyers tend to prepare a document in draft and submit the draft to the solicitor acting for the other person involved. So simple is the form of TRANSFER OF WHOLE that there is not much room for argument about how it should be worded; the stage of submitting the deed in draft is therefore often dispensed with.

Matthew prepared four copies of the transfer. Two of them he sent to Dodds & Son. The top copy would be used as an engrossment. Therefore he stuck red stickers over the word 'seal' on the back page of the form against where Mr and Mrs Timms would sign. He kept one copy for his own file. The fourth copy he would send shortly to Hodgson, Green & Co, acting for his building society.

replies to requisitions

Dodds & Son replied to Matthew's letter of 12 February:

DODDS & SON
Solicitors

1 Charter Street
Minford, Surrey

17 February 1986

To: M. J. Seaton Esq

Dear Sir,

Re: 14 Twintree Avenue, Minford

We now return your requisitions on title, together with our replies. We approve the form of draft transfer, and, in accordance with your suggestion, are treating the top copy as the engrossment, and shall have this executed by our clients. We are obliged to you for the spare copies of the requisitions and of the transfer which you have sent for our file.

We shall be in touch with you again nearer completion date.

Yours faithfully,
DODDS & SON

Dodds & Son's answers to Matthew's requisitions on title were satisfactory. They confirmed that their answers to the preliminary enquiries still stood, and that suitable evidence about payment of rates and other outgoings would be produced at completion. A completion statement would be sent nearer the date for completion.

They confirmed that the existing mortgage in favour of the Minford Building Society would be paid off and added that if form 53 could not be handed over on completion they would give an unqualified undertaking. This meant that if the building society holding the Timms' mortgage could not provide the official form saying that the mortgage was paid off, they (Dodds & Son or the seller's building society's solicitors) would give a personal and unqualified undertaking to send the form without delay. Dodds & Son also confirmed that there was no one other than Mr and Mrs Timms in occupation of the property and that vacant possession would be given at completion. Arrangements about handing over the keys to the house would be made later. Finally they said that they would defer until later saying where completion would take place and how and to whom the money should be paid.

the building society's solicitors

Matthew was now ready to contact Hodgson, Green & Co, the solicitors acting for the Forthright Building Society, his mortgagees.

38 Broadstone Drive
Hastings, Sussex

18 February 1986

To: Messrs Hodgson, Green & Co

Dear Sirs,

Re: 14 Twintree Avenue, Minford

Further to your letter of 3 February, I now enclose the following:

(i) contract dated 7 February 1986
(ii) enquiries before contract, including supplementary enquiries, and replies
(iii) local land charges search certificate and enquiries of the local authority, with replies
(iv) office copies of the entries on the register and filed plan
(v) requisitions on title and replies
(vi) draft transfer as approved by the sellers' solicitors
(vii) an authority for you to inspect the register.

I look forward to receiving your requisitions and the mortgage deed. The agreed completion date is 7 March: no doubt you will arrange to have the money available then.

Yours faithfully,
M. J. Seaton

A buyer who is anxious about his building society's approval for his mortgage loan might have sent to them earlier, before exchange of contract, his preliminary enquiries with replies, the local land charges search certificate and the enquiries of the local authority with replies, and the office copies of the entries on the register and filed plan and would now send the rest of the required documents.

Matthew was about to part with some of the most important documents concerning his purchase and would probably never see them again because a building society keeps all the documents, as a rule. He therefore had photocopies made of them, to keep on his file. He also made a separate note of the date when the office copy of the entries on the register was issued from the Land Registry – 10 January 1986. He would need to have this date at hand when filling his application for an official search of the register, nearer completion.

Matthew had a reply from Hodgson, Green & Co by return of post:

HODGSON, GREEN & CO
Solicitors

67 Lomax Street
Minford, Surrey

20 February 1986

Dear Sir,

Re: 14 Twintree Avenue, Minford

Thank you for your letter of 18 February with enclosures. We now enclose our requisitions on title for your attention. We further enclose the engrossed mortgage deed for execution by you, together with a copy for your use. The mortgage deed is in standard form and our clients permit no variations from it. You will see that the deed bears an endorsement, a Declaration and Request in the agreed form, for signature by your wife and any other person who will be in occupation of the house at the date of completion of the mortgage advance. The Declaration and Request should be signed in the presence of a witness.

We await your replies to our requisitions.

Yours faithfully,
HODGSON, GREEN & CO

the building society's requisitions on title

Building societies' requisitions are a list of questions about the house you are buying, covering the same sort of points as your preliminary enquiries and requisitions on title. As far as possible, you should use the seller's solicitor's replies to these, to answer the building society's requisitions. Then, if need be, you will have to ask the seller's solicitor to answer any outstanding questions.

There is no standard form in common use by building societies for these requisitions. Different solicitors use different forms; sometimes they are printed or duplicated. It may also happen that no requisitions at all are asked, if the title is registered with title absolute; any points which need to be dealt with are raised in a letter.

Hodgson, Green & Co had framed their own questions. The questions asked, and the answers Matthew gave, were as follows:

REQUISITIONS ON TITLE

Seaton – and *Forthright Building Society*
14 Twintree Avenue, Minford

1. Please confirm that the borrower is finding the full amount of the purchase price, apart from this mortgage loan, out of his own funds.	1. *I so confirm.*
2. Please confirm that the borrower is obtaining full vacant possession of the property on completion and that no lettings of any kind are contemplated.	2. *I so confirm.*
3(a). Please give the names of all persons aged 18 or over (or approaching that age) not being parties to the mortgage deed, who will be in, or will enter into, occupation of the property at the date of completion of the mortgage.	3(a). *My wife, Emma Seaton.*
3(b). Please confirm that any such person or persons will execute a Declaration and Request, to be endorsed upon the mortgage, postponing any interest or claim they may have in or against the property to the society's mortgage.	3(b). *Confirmed.*

4. Where will completion take place?
5. We shall require to receive on completion the following:
   1) Charge certificate
   2) Form 53 duly executed or undertaking
   3) Transfer duly executed by vendor
   4) Land Registry Form A4 duly completed
   5) Form Stamps L(A)451 duly completed
   6) Mortgage Deed duly executed in the presence of a solicitor, with any requisite Declaration and Request signed by any intended occupant.
   7) Search Certificate (94A) not more than 10 days old.

Dated *20 February 1986*

4. *I am enquiring.*
5. *Noted.*
   With regard to my execution of the mortgage deed, as you know I am not represented. Would it suffice if I were to execute the mortgage deed at completion, in the presence of your representative attending completion? If not, what do you suggest?

Dated *21 February 1986*

the rest of the money

Building societies often like to know that a buyer himself is providing the whole of the rest of the money, that is the difference between the price and the amount borrowed. They feel that if the borrower has a sufficient stake of his own in the property, he is less likely to default on the mortgage.

A question asking the buyer to confirm his own stake in the purchase may have appeared on the application for mortgage form. If a buyer is borrowing elsewhere, they like to be informed and it will be the responsibility of the building society's solicitors to ensure that any subsequent charges are registered with the knowledge and consent of the building society.

no other interested parties

Question 2 firstly asked Matthew to confirm that he was obtaining full vacant possession on completion. The building society, like the buyer, has to ensure that it will not be prejudicially affected by the interests or claims of any person who was in occupation of the property with the seller before completion. The building society also likes to know that only the borrower and his family will be occupying the house; hence the reference to lettings. Understandably, the society does not want to be landed with tenants they cannot get rid of, especially those with full Rent

Act protection. If the borrower defaults on his mortgage payments, and the society has to sell the house, it is worth far less with tenants in it than with vacant possession. In fact, the terms of the society's offer of advance usually state that no lettings may be made. The question merely required formal confirmation.

As well as making sure that it is not bound by the rights of anyone living in the property with the seller before completion, a building society has to be sure that it will not be bound by the rights of any person who is intending to occupy the property with the borrower. That is why the building society asks question 3 and requires any such person to sign a 'declaration and request' (or other form of consent, or release, or postponement) to be endorsed on the mortgage, postponing (that is, not enforcing) any rights they may have in the property. Emma was the only person who was going to move into 14 Twintree Avenue with Matthew and she was quite happy to sign such a document.

The society could have made it a requirement that Emma sign the declaration and request in the presence of her own solicitor. They did not do so because it was extremely unlikely that Emma could successfully claim, after the mortgage was granted, that the document she had signed was void for undue influence even though at the time she signed it she was not legally represented. To establish a claim of undue influence, she would have to prove that the transaction was to her substantial disadvantage. Matthew's borrowing the necessary finance to buy their new home could hardly be said to be to her disadvantage, substantial or otherwise – nor in fact to the disadvantage of any wife or other member of a buyer's family in a similar position. The only time undue influence is a real risk to a mortgagee is where a person wants to borrow money on the security of a house he already owns, for a purpose other than its initial purchase. Nevertheless a note at the bottom of the *Declaration and Request* endorsed on the mortgage deed advises the occupant to consult a solicitor if he or she is not clear of the legal implications in executing it. Emma recognised the legal implications involved. She would sign it in front of her neighbour, as witness, one day next week. Matthew should not witness her signature, lest it appear that Emma had been coerced by him to sign the consent.

where will completion take place

Question 4 asked where completion would be taking place. Matthew was not sure at the moment. The general rule is that completion takes place at the office of the seller's solicitor or of the solicitor acting for the seller's building society or other mortgagee. This is confirmed by Law Society general condition 21(1) and National condition 5(4). Or it may be made by post – but not if the buyer is acting without a solicitor.

Matthew knew that Mr and Mrs Timms had a mortgage with the Minford Building Society which would be paid off on completion. He assumed, therefore, that completion would take place at the offices of Minford Building Society's solicitors, but as yet he did not know who or where they were. If the Timms' had had no mortgage, completion would have taken place at the offices of Dodds & Son. The undertaking about form 53, if one was to be provided, would come from Minford Building Society's solicitors and would provide that the form should be made available to Hodgson, Green & Co within 14 days of completion.

Finally, the list of documents which Hodgson, Green & Co would require at completion was set out at this stage to avoid any misunderstanding later.

An unusual problem presented itself at this stage: the Forthright Building Society required that the mortgage deed be executed in the presence of a solicitor, who would sign it as the witness. Although there is no requirement in law that the deed must be witnessed by a solicitor, some building societies still make this their requirement. Where a buyer is legally represented, his own solicitor is normally witness to the borrower's execution of the mortgage deed. He usually executes it some time before completion, although it does not become operative until then.

Matthew had suggested that he should execute the deed when he personally attended completion. He could then execute in the presence of the solicitor from Hodgson, Green & Co who attended completion. Alternatively, he could have taken it into any solicitor's office and executed there. Solicitors will witness the execution of a document on payment of a small fee (perhaps £3).

the mortgage deed

Building societies and other institutional lenders use standard forms of mortgage deeds which contain the details, terms and conditions. They are all worded slightly differently, because each building society or other lender has its own particular standard form of mortgage. The standard mortgage clauses are generally quite easy to understand. If you do not fully understand what any clause says, ask the building society's solicitors to explain it to you.

Often the mortgage deed is a very simply worded document, containing a reference to a separate leaflet or booklet setting out the conditions.

The mortgage deed Matthew received was in the normal form for the Forthright Building Society. It was a printed document with some blank spaces in it, mainly at the beginning and the end which had been filled in with details special to his purchase.

Matthew checked that his name had been spelt correctly, that the property was correctly described and that the amount of the mortgage advance, the rate of interest and the monthly payments corresponded with the mortgage offer. He also noted that many of the clauses referred to the matters mentioned in the society's offer of advance of 31 January. Thus there was a clause enabling the society to alter the rate of interest on giving notice, one forbidding the borrower letting the property and one requiring the borrower to insure the property 'for the cost of reinstatement' with a company to be approved by the society.

A borrower should check from his mortgage deed, or from the mortgage provisions if separately printed, whether the building society's consent is required to his taking out a second mortgage elsewhere.

The embargo on amendments to a society's standard mortgage deed is quite usual. You either have to take it or leave it. Hence the practice of sending the engrossment of the mortgage deed (with a copy) straight away, cutting out the draft stage. If you are sent a draft mortgage deed for approval, the request for your approval is only a formality and you may not even be required to send back the top copy approved; in such a case you will only receive one copy of the draft deed. When you have given your token approval, the engrossed mortgage deed will be sent to you for execution.

Matthew returned Hodgson, Green & Co's requisitions straight away with the following letter:

38 Broadstone Drive
Hastings, Sussex

21 February 1986

To: Messrs Hodgson, Green & Co

Dear Sirs,

Re: 14 Twintree Avenue, Minford

Thank you for your letter of 21 February enclosing the mortgage deed and requisitions, and for the copies for my file. I now return my replies to your requisitions.

I shall be grateful if you will let me know as soon as possible the amount that will be available on completion after deducting expenses.

Yours faithfully,
M. J. Seaton

It is a good idea to retain a copy of the mortgage deed in your file. The executed mortgage deed will be kept by the building society (or other lender) after completion.

asking for a completion statement

Dodds & Son had still not supplied Matthew with the detailed arrangements for completion. He wrote them this reminder:

38 Broadstone Drive
Hastings, Sussex

24 February 1986

To: Messrs Dodds & Son

Dear Sirs,

Re: 14 Twintree Avenue, Minford

I refer to your letter of 17 February, and shall be obliged if you will let me have a completion statement for 7 March as soon as possible.

Presumably you will require the sum to be paid in the form of a banker's draft.

Please arrange for the keys to be handed over at completion, or if more convenient to be left with the estate agents.

Can you now let me know where completion will take place?

Yours faithfully,
M. J. Seaton

It is the usual practice between solicitors to carry out the financial side of the transfer of property by banker's draft. This is recognised by both sets of conditions of sale. Law Society general condition 21(2)(b) provides that the draft must be drawn by and upon a CHAPS settlement bank (which Matthew's bank, Lloyds Bank plc, was). In the National conditions, condition 5(3) says that the banker's draft must be issued by a "designated bank". The list of designated banks is wider than the CHAPS settlement banks and includes most commercial banks.

telegraphic transfer

Sometimes it is necessary or desirable to have a sale and a purchase completed at the same time, so that the money received from the sale of the old house can be used towards the purchase of the new one, and the buyer can move out of his old and into his new home on the same day.

This operation is relatively simple if the parties are within easy reach of each other. Where the sale is governed by the Law Society conditions, the sale can be completed in the morning, the draft for the money received paid into a CHAPS settlement bank and a new draft drawn for the purchase of the buyer's new home in the afternoon. The CHAPS system provides for the immediate clearance of drafts. Alternatively, the draft for the money received from the sale can be endorsed over to the seller at the afternoon completion.

Where the parties are too distant from each other for this procedure to be carried out, a buyer's solicitor can complete the purchase by 'credit or telegraphic transfer'.

The procedure is as follows: the buyer's solicitor obtains details of the seller's solicitor's bank and the number of the account (called a client account) into which he pays clients' money and arranges for the completion money to be paid direct to that account by credit transfer from his bank to the other. The seller's solicitor's bank is asked to telephone its customer the minute the credit is received. The seller's solicitor then telephones the buyer's solicitor to confirm that the funds are released and that completion can take place, and will then telephone the selling agents advising them that completion has taken place and asking them to release the keys to the buyer. The completion documents are then sent through the post. One criticism levelled at this method of transmitting funds is that it can cause a delay in completion if an account is credited later than the time set for completion. This problem is avoided if both the seller's and buyer's solicitors are CHAPS customers – the electronic system guarantees same-day credit.

It is not recommended that a buyer attempts these methods without a solicitor (even if he has the necessary money and does not have to rely on a solicitor's undertaking to obtain bridging finance) mainly because of the inherent danger of something not being quite right in the documents, or the very remote possibility of the seller's solicitor absconding with the purchase money, in which case the buyer would have to bear the loss. The buyer's solicitor and the buyer are protected against these dangers by the new Law Society's Code for Completion by Post, the layman is not.

the building society's solicitors reply

Matthew had a reply from Hodgson, Green & Co:

HODGSON, GREEN & CO
Solicitors

67 Lomax Street
Minford, Surrey

26 February 1986

To: M. J. Seaton Esq

Dear Sir,

Re: 14 Twintree Avenue, Minford

We thank you for your letter of 21 February. With regard to your query on the execution of the mortgage deed, it will be quite in order if you execute it at completion in the presence of the writer, assuming of course that completion takes place in this town. If it does not, it would be necessary for you to make an alternative arrangement about executing the mortgage.

We enclose a statement showing £31,168.25 as being available on completion, after deducting the expenses shown. If it is required that this sum be provided in split drafts, please let us know as soon as possible, and in any event not later than 3 days before completion, the amount of each draft and to whom it should be payable.

We enclose a copy of the Society's rules for your retention.

Yours faithfully,
HODGSON, GREEN & CO

Hodgson, Green & Co enclosed a copy of the Forthright Building Society's rules for Matthew to keep. He had, in fact, got a copy of these already as he had been saving with the society for some years and was an established member. If he is not one already, a potential borrower must become a member of the society that will lend him money, but such membership is little more than a formality.

what will be deducted

Rather more important for the moment was the statement which Hodgson, Green & Co sent with their letter showing how much of the loan would be left after the expenses had been deducted.

SEATON AND FORTHRIGHT BUILDING SOCIETY
Re: 14 Twintree Avenue, Minford, Surrey

		£	£
	Mortgage advance		32,000.00
	Deductions:		
1)	Stamp duty on transfer at £46,000	460.00	
2)	Land Registry fees	105.00	
3)	Our costs (fees, searches, charges, VAT)	167.75	
4)	Insurance premium	99.00	
	less		831.75
	Net sum available on completion		31,168.25

The expenses were deducted from his mortgage advance because after completion Hodgson, Green & Co would take away the transfer, mortgage deed and other documents which were their client society's security for the loan. They would attend to the stamping of the transfer, and the registration of it and of the mortgage at the Land Registry. Where title to property is registered, the buyer has to register the transfer of ownership to him (otherwise the legal title to the property does not vest in him) and is charged a fee for doing this. Land Registry fees are on a scale and the amounts depend on the purchase price. The mortgage is also registered but no fee is charged for doing this if it is done at the same time as registering the change of proprietorship. The stamp duty and Land Registry fees would be paid by Hodgson, Green & Co but were Matthew's responsibility; hence the deduction.

Hodgson, Green & Co's legal costs were also his responsibility. Matthew had been told in the offer of advance that he would have to bear their costs. There is a scale of fees recommended jointly by the Law Society and the Building Societies Association to be paid to a solicitor who deals with the legal side of a building society mortgage and is also acting for the buyer. Where the buyer is doing his own conveyancing and a solicitor is acting for the building society only, he must also charge whatever is a 'fair and reasonable' fee or a fee on a scale recommended by the Building Societies Association.

Finally, the insurance premium was deducted. The house had been insured with the Bridstow Insurance Company since exchange of contracts. To make sure that the property was insured, the society had paid the first premium and deducted it from their loan. The insurance had been based on the reinstatement value of the house, that is the cost of rebuilding it should it be totally destroyed, not its present market value. Thus 14 Twintree Avenue was insured for £55,000 not £46,000.

The Bridstow Insurance Company charged an annual premium at the rate of 18p per £100 for their buildings insurance on a house in Surrey. On £55,000 this worked out as £99 p.a.

completion statement

On friday, Matthew had a letter from Dodds & Son:

DODDS & SON
Solicitors

1 Charter Street
Minford, Surrey

27 February 1986

To: M. J. Seaton Esq

Dear Sir,

Re: 14 Twintree Avenue, Minford

We now enclose a completion statement for 7 March. Completion will take place at the offices of Messrs Anderson, James & Pringle, 88 Great Winchester Street, Minford, solicitors for the existing mortgagees. We confirm that the balance required to complete must be paid by banker's draft and split as indicated in the note on the completion statement. We have noted what you say about keys.

Yours faithfully,
DODDS & SON

The completion statement read as follows:

TIMMS TO SEATON
14 TWINTREE AVENUE, MINFORD, SURREY
COMPLETION STATEMENT
as at 7th March 1986

	£
Purchase price	46,000.00
Less deposit	4,600.00
Balance payable on completion	41,400.00

Please provide above sum in two drafts in favour of:
(1) Minford Building Society for £7,738.08
(2) Ourselves (Dodds & Son) for £33,661.92

The seller's solicitor sends the buyer or his solicitor a completion statement showing the amount he will require on completion, about a week before completion. Where relevant, such a statement would also deal with outgoings and apportionments.

outgoings

The general rule is that the seller is responsible for outgoings up to and including the day of completion, thereafter they must be borne by the buyer. In legal circles 'outgoings' are thought of as including general rate, water rate, sewerage charge, also ground rent and service charges under a lease.

Rates – that is, general rate, water rate and sewerage charge – are payable by the occupier of the property and it is quite clear that a buyer cannot be made to pay arrears of rates unpaid by the seller. Law Society general condition 19(2) provides that rates should not be apportioned. This means that the seller is not entitled to deduct from the purchase price any sum he has paid in advance in respect of rates; nor need he make the buyer an allowance where the rates are payable in arrear. Instead, the seller or his solicitor will write to the rating authorities informing them of the sale and the completion date, with the full name of the buyer and asking for an apportioned figure for the seller up to completion. There is an official form (46A) which can be used for this. If the outgoings have been paid in advance, the seller will get a refund.

If the National Conditions of Sale were used, rates can be apportioned on completion and the completion statement would show the sum required to complete as:

purchase price,
less deposit,
plus or minus an apportionment of general and water rate and sewerage charge (depending on whether at the date of completion it is in arrears or has been paid in advance).

But even where the sale is governed by the National Conditions it is more usual to let the local authority apportion the rates. (This is particularly so where the property has been empty for a while and there are no rates payable for some period up to completion.)

In fact, where a completion statement is as simple as Matthew's it is often dispensed with. The seller's solicitor simply informs the buyer by letter of the amount required to complete.

In the case of leasehold property, the ground rent and any service charges payable to the landlord and the annual insurance premium (although strictly speaking, not an outgoing) will be apportioned on completion and be shown on the completion statement. Ground rent is usually paid to the landlord in advance on each quarter day or half-yearly. As a rule, the insurance premium has to be apportioned because the buyer has no option but to take over the existing policy if the lease so requires. The apportionment of the insurance premium is made from exchange of contracts, when the property started to be at the buyer's risk.

As far as electricity and gas are concerned, the seller should arrange to have the meters read on the day he gives possession to the buyer. If the telephone belongs to British Telecom and is being taken over, they should be asked to apportion the rental.

how much to whom

The completion statement will tell you how the seller's solicitor wants the purchase money to be paid: all by way of banker's draft in his favour or some of it in favour of another firm, for example the seller's building society's solicitor. This is where matters can become complicated for a buyer, because you have to bring the right amounts of money with you to completion. The difficulty does not derive from the law but from the diversity of most buyers' financial resources. For example, you may be buying a house with the aid of a building society mortgage and provide the balance from the sale of your present house, out of the proceeds of which you have to pay off an existing mortgage; your seller's solicitor has asked for two drafts: one in his favour and one in favour of the seller's building society.

It is really a question of sitting down and working out where the money is coming from and going to. It may help to remember that if part of your purchase price is coming from the proceeds of a simultaneous sale of your own house, then, provided that the banker's draft you get on your sale is in your favour and not crossed 'account payee only', you can use it for your purchase (by endorsing it) without having to put it through your bank. Alternatively, you can ask your buyer's solicitor to split the money for your house into two separate banker's drafts if required by your seller's solicitor, or possibly into three if you have an existing mortgage to pay off.

Matthew's financial calculations were going to be relatively simple because he had only been asked for two drafts: one in favour of the Minford Building Society which would be used to discharge Mr and Mrs Timms' mortgage, and the other (for the balance) in favour of Dodds & Son.

If by any chance you have paid a preliminary deposit ('earnest money') to the seller's estate agent, the completion statement will also require you to produce a deposit release at completion. This can be in the form of a simple letter addressed to the agent asking him to release the deposit to the seller.

practical matters

It was a very busy time for Matthew and the legal side of the purchase was not the only matter that was taking up his time. There was also the sorting and packing and clearing out of the rented flat they were living in, arranging for removal men, for having the meters read, getting change of address cards prepared and sent off and all the other rigmarole of getting ready for moving. He transferred £10,000 from his savings into his current account at the bank, so that he would not have any difficulties when it came to paying out at completion.

That weekend he learnt on the telephone from Mr and Mrs Timms that they had arranged to move out of 14 Twintree Avenue on 6 March, so that the house would be ready for the Seatons on the 7th. Unless a special arrangement is made, the seller does not let a buyer take possession until completion has actually taken place and the money handed over. There might be a last-minute hitch which could conceivably result in the sale never being completed; things might then be awkward for the seller if the buyer had already moved in.

It is, however, very important for the buyer to make sure that the house has been totally vacated before handing over the purchase money, and that there is no one in the house. If your contract incorporates the National conditions of sale, you have the right, on giving reasonable notice to the seller or his solicitor, to insist that you or your representative be given possession of the property immediately before completion.

completion time

It is a good idea to arrange (if you can) to have the keys before completion, so that you can inspect the house on completion day. Mr and Mrs Timms would not agree to give Matthew the keys early but they did promise to arrange for Flint & Morgan to let Matthew into the house on the morning of 7 March.

Matthew wrote to Dodds & Son:

38 Broadstone Drive
Hastings, Sussex

1 March 1986

To: Messrs Dodds & Son

Dear Sirs,

Re: 14 Twintree Avenue, Minford

Thank you for your letter of 28 February enclosing the completion statement. I note that the amount required to complete is £41,400 of which £7,738.08 is to go to the Minford Building Society.

I understand that your clients are moving out on 6 March and that the keys will be handed over by you at completion. Is this right?

I shall be moving in during the afternoon of 7 March, all being well. An appointment for completion at, say, 12 noon would suit me. Would you let me know whether this is acceptable to yourselves and Messrs Anderson, James & Pringle? The solicitors acting for my mortgagees, Messrs Hodgson, Green & Co, are able to fit in with this suggestion.

Yours faithfully,
M. J. Seaton

The special conditions in your contract will usually give a latest time for completion on the day in question, otherwise it counts as a working day later. This is to ease the financial arrangements of the parties. Special condition B of Matthew's contract said that completion should take place by 2.0 p.m. on friday 7 March. If the special conditions are silent on the matter, Law Society general condition 21(5)(a) states that completion should take place by 2.30 p.m. on the day in question. National condition 5(5)(i) mentions completion time only for a friday: if it does not take place by 2.15 p.m., it is deemed to take place the following monday.

Matthew had telephoned Hodgson, Green & Co on friday afternoon, informing them of the venue for completion. 12 noon had been a suitable time for them, and he subsequently heard that it was also convenient for Dodds & Son and Anderson, James & Pringle.

Matthew wrote to Hodgson, Green & Co mainly to confirm what he had already told them on the telephone:

38 Broadstone Drive
Hastings, Sussex

1 March 1986

To: Messrs Hodgson, Green & Co

Dear Sirs,

Re: 14 Twintree Avenue, Minford

I have your letter of 25 February and note what you say regarding the execution of the mortgage.

I have now received a completion statement from the sellers' solicitors and can tell you how the amount to be made available at completion should be split. Please provide the sum of £31,168.25 in two drafts as follows:

1) in favour of Minford Building Society £ 7,738.08
2) in favour of Dodds & Son £23,430.17

I confirm our telephone conservation to the effect that completion is to take place at the offices of Messrs Anderson, James & Pringle of 88 Great Winchester Street, Minford on 7th March. The suggested time for completion is 12 noon. I will let you know when and if this time is confirmed.

Yours faithfully,
M. J. Seaton

This meant that Matthew would only have to request one draft from his bank: for £10,231.75 in favour of Dodds & Son, to make up the balance of the amount due on completion of £41,400.

He subsequently telephoned Hodgson, Green & Co to confirm that completion would take place at 12 noon.

notes in preparation for completion

On sunday, Matthew prepared for his own use a memorandum for completion:

14 Twintree Avenue: completion at 12 noon on 7th March 1986 at Anderson, James & Pringle, 88 Great Winchester Street, Minford.

I take with me:
- Official search certificate (form 94A)
- Land Registry application (form A4)
- Stamps L(A) 451 form
- mortgage deed (with declaration and request on back signed by Emma)
- my banker's draft payable to Dodds & Son for £10,231.75
- receipt for deposit of £4,600 (letter from Dodds & Son of 7 February 1986)

Hodgson, Green & Co (acting for Forthright Building Society) will require from me:
- official search certificate (form 94A)
- Land Registry application (form A4)
- Stamps L(A)451 form
- mortgage deed with declaration and request signed by Emma.

Hodgson, Green & Co will require from Anderson, James & Pringle (acting for Minford Building Society):
- charge certificate
- form 53 or an undertaking to discharge the existing mortgage.

Hodgson, Green & Co will require from Dodds & Son (acting for Mr and Mrs Timms):
- transfer executed by Mr and Mrs Timms.

Dodds & Son (acting for Mr and Mrs Timms) will require from me:
- banker's draft for £10,231.75.

They will require from Hodgson, Green & Co:
- banker's draft for £23,430.17.

Anderson, James & Pringle (acting for Minford Building Society) will require from Hodgson, Green & Co:
- banker's draft for £7,738.08.

I will require from Dodds & Son: keys, and to see receipts for general rate, water rate and sewerage charge.

Money (i.e. banker's drafts)	£	£
from me		10,231.75
from Forthright Building Society	7,738.08	
from Forthright Building Society	23,430.17	31,168.25
due per completion statement		41,400.00
Split thus:		
to Minford BS (from Forthright BS)		7,738.08
to Dodds & Son (from Forthright BS)		23,430.17
to Dodds & Son (from me)		10,231.75
		41,400.00

The memorandum set out the essence of what would happen on completion. It served a double function: a reminder to Matthew, and a summary of the financial side of the purchase.

He also wrote down, as a note to himself, the other costs involved, which came to over £1,000.

	£
Stamp duty on transfer	460.00
Land Registry fees	105.00
Hodgson, Green & Co's fees & charges	167.75
Insurance premium	99.00
Building society valuation fee	69.00
Own survey fee	160.00
Local search fees	15.10

official search

Monday 3 March was ringed in red in Matthew's diary; he had to send off his application for an official search of the register at the Land Registry.

The search is done on form 94A if you are buying the whole of the land comprised in the title; form 94B if you are buying part only (say one house in ten). An application on form 94B must usually be accompanied by a plan. Both forms are simple to fill in if you follow their wording and instructions carefully.

Matthew used form 94A. At the top of the form was a box for the name of the district land registry to which the form was being sent. It is important to send it to the right one. There is a list of district land registries on the back of form 94A and B (with telephone numbers). If you are still not sure which district land registry covers the district in which you are buying your house, telephone any one of these for the information. Surrey is covered by Tunbridge Wells, so Matthew sent his form there.

Underneath, the first three sections required details of the county and district, title number of the property and full names of the registered proprietors. Matthew took these off the copy of the office copy entries on the register which he had made earlier. The fourth section is the crunch one. It read: "Application is made to ascertain whether any adverse entry has been made in the register since the date shown opposite being EITHER the date on which an office copy of the subsisting entries in the register was issued OR the last date of which the land or charge certificate was officially examined with the register." The date required here is that shown on the bottom of the office copy entries: in Matthew's case, 10 January 1986.

In the unlikely event of your having been supplied with an ordinary copy (not an office copy) of the seller's title, it will have a date written on it by the seller's solicitor, namely the date of the inside cover of the actual land or charge certificate. This is the date on which the land or charge certificate was last examined and brought up to date by the Land Registry and is the date that should be inserted on the form. Alternatively, the seller's solicitor will have supplied you with this date in answer to question 3(B) of your requisitions on title.

In the fifth section Matthew wrote his full name: he was the applicant for the search. The sixth section only applies where a solicitor is making the search on the buyer's behalf.

Underneath this Matthew had to put an X in box B (which applied where the applicant was not a solicitor) to indicate that the written authority of the registered proprietors, Mr and Mrs Timms, to inspect the register accompanied the form. Without such authority the buyer cannot make his search. At the bottom of the form was a space to fill in the name and address to which the form should be sent. Matthew filled in his own. The "key number" box is inapplicable.

The form has a tear-off duplicate which must also be filled in, the original being returned to the applicant with the certificate on the back date-stamped by the Land Registry.

The search form is a device to warn you of any adverse entries which may have been put on the register since the date of the office copy entries, or when the land or charge certificate was last officially compared with the register. It is essential for the buyer to have obtained the official search certificate back from the Land Registry before completion takes place. He should never complete without it.

When the Land Registry sends back an official search certificate, it confirms that no adverse entry has been made since the date searched from. If it says something other than this, do not complete. Refer back to pages 52 to 57 for the action to be taken regarding the entry.

A building society will not release its loan without an official search certificate. The building society's solicitors will probably have carried out a similar search.

priority

The search certificate says another thing, namely that if the buyer applies to be the registered owner before 11 a.m. on the thirtieth working day from the date of the certificate, no adverse entry (including the registration of someone else as owner) can be registered against the title in the mean time. This is what is meant by saying that a search gives a priority period of thirty working days.

So the time factor is extremely important in the case of an official search of the register.

The search should be sent off about 4 or 5 working days before completion: ideally the certificate should be dated the day before completion. The point of this is to ensure that the buyer gets the full benefit of the period of priority which his certificate of search gives him.

Sending off the search form as near to completion as possible also allows the maximum possible time after completion to attend to the stamping of the transfer (where necessary) and other formalities and to lodge the application to register the transfer before the priority period expires.

The Land Registry is usually reliable about searches, and district land registries send their replies by first class mail, often by return of post, to all applications for research received by first post. You can telephone the district land registry concerned to find out what is the current delay in dealing with searches. You should allow a few days longer for the return of a form 96B search.

In an emergency, a search can be made in person. This is rarely done because a personal search gives the buyer no protection whatsoever. If the Land Registry makes a mistake in a postal application for an official search and the buyer suffers loss, he is entitled to be compensated. But a buyer who makes a personal search is not entitled to be indemnified nor does he get the priority protection mentioned above.

If there is a significant delay in completing your purchase you should make a second search to ensure that completion takes place and the application to register the transfer is lodged with a priority period in the buyer's and his mortgagee's favour.

Matthew posted form 94A (first class) together with his authority to inspect the register which (Dodds & Son had sent him with their letter of 7 February) to Tunbridge Wells District Land Registry. No fee is payable for the search.

"bankruptcy only" search

Another official search which the building society's solicitor may undertake and which sometimes a buyer may be asked to make is a "bankruptcy only" search in the Land Charges Registry. This is in Plymouth and is quite distinct from the Land Registry at Lincoln's Inn Fields, London and the district land registries.

Usually a search in the Land Charges Registry is only made by, or on behalf of, a buyer of unregistered land. However a building society may ask even a buyer of registered land to make a search in certain of the registers kept in the Land Charges Registry, namely the registers of pending actions, writs and orders, and deeds of arrangement. Such a search, called a "bankruptcy only" search, will reveal something the search on form 94A or B will not reveal, namely whether the buyer has been or is likely to be made bankrupt. This is of obvious interest to a building society lending thousands of pounds. A "bankruptcy only" search in the Land Charges Registry gives 15 working days' priority.

The application to the Land Charges Registry is made on form K16, a pink form; the only information sought is whether or not the buyer is bankrupt. The name and address of the applicant must be filled in and the forenames and surname to be searched. In this case, it would have been 'Matthew John Seaton': it is the buyer against whom the search is being made; in fact, the buyer is applying for a search against himself. The fee for making the search is 50p per name (so if the property is bought in joint names, it would be £1) and a cheque or postal order for this amount should accompany your application for search. The result (certificate) of the search will be returned by the Land Charges Registry within 3 to 4 days either to your address or the one you give in the right hand panel (the building society's solicitors).

It is possible to get a telephone search (with confirmation of the results within 24 hours) but only for someone (such as Oyez and most solicitors) who has credit facilities with the Land Charges Registry. A "bankruptcy only" search cannot be made personally.

Some building societies' solicitors mention bankruptcy clearance as part of their normal requisitions; for some, their solicitors do it; some do not bother with it. Matthew had not been asked to supply a "bankruptcy only" search.

While he was filling in forms he thought he might as well fill in the other two, form A4 and the Stamps L(A) 451 form that would have to be ready to be handed over to Hodgson, Green & Co at completion.

preparing form A4

A buyer becomes the full legal owner of registered property when when his application to be registered as the new proprietor is received at the Land Registry, not when the property is actually transferred to him on completion. The Land Registration Act lays down no time-limit within which a buyer must apply to be registered as the new proprietor, but to take advantage of the priority period conferred by his official certificate of search, a buyer should lodge his application for registration before the thirty day period expires. Since an interval of several weeks elapses between the date of application for registration and the actual date of registration and the buyer must be protected from any intermediate dealings with the property by the seller, registration is deemed to take place on the date the application for registration is delivered to the Land Registry.

The buyer applies to the Land Registry to have his name entered as the registered proprietor on form A4 *Application to register dealings with the whole of titles.* If buying part of land with registered title, use form A5, which is in similar terms. Form A4 consists of four pages; page 3 is for Land Registry use only, on the other pages you have to fill in the white 'boxes' only.

On the front page, in box 1 you should insert the title number of the property. Box 2 requires the applicant to state the nature of applications in priority order. Matthew was in fact making three applications; first the removal, or discharge, of Mr and Mrs Timms' mortgage; secondly, Matthew's name to be substituted for Mr and Mrs Timms as the name of the registered proprietor; and thirdly, details of Matthew's mortgage to the Forthright Building Society to be entered on the charges register. He therefore filled in this part of the form as follows:

Nature of applications in priority order	Value £	Fee scale para or abatement	Fees paid £
Discharge of mortgage	—	—	
Transfer	*£46,000*	*4*	*105.00*
Mortgage	*£32,000*	*abatement*	
		Total	*105.00*

No fee is payable on the discharge of a mortgage. The Land Registry fee for a transfer is charged according to 'Land Registry fee scale 4' calculated on the price of the house. The value of the buyer's mortgage must be stated, but where a mortgage and transfer are registered simultaneously, the normal Land Registry fee for a mortgage is reduced ('abated') to nil; "abatement" should be inserted in column three.

Next, box 3 asks for a list of all documents lodged with the application. Matthew listed: charge certificate, form 53, transfer, official search certificate on form 94A, mortgage deed and copy of the mortgage deed. The Land Registry require a certified copy (this is a copy which a solicitor certifies to be a true one) of the mortgage to be lodged with the application. Hodgson, Green & Co would provide a certified copy for this purpose.

Box 4 asks for the name and address of the person or firm lodging the application to whom any requisitions will be sent and to whom documents (including land certificate or charge certificate) should be returned. Where the buyer buys with the help of a mortgage, the application is sent or lodged with the Land Registry by the lender or the lender's solicitor. Matthew wrote there the name and address of Hodgson, Green & Co. If you are buying without the aid of a mortgage, insert your own name and address so that the land certificate can be sent to you eventually.

Sometimes a document lodged with an application to the Land Registry has to be returned to someone other than the applicant after the Land Registry has dealt with the application, for instance if it deals with other property as well as that to which the application relates. This is unlikely to be the case with property within the scope of this book; box 5 should be left blank.

At the bottom of the front page the applicant is told to turn to page 4 (on the back of the form) and complete panels 6 and 7.

Panel 6 asks for the full name and address of the new proprietor of the land. Matthew inserted there: MATTHEW JOHN SEATON, accountant, of 14 TWINTREE AVENUE, MINFORD, SURREY". Since he would be moving into 14 Twintree Avenue immediately after completion that was the address he used.

Panel 7 requested details of the proprietor of the new charge.

In here Matthew wrote the full name and address of the Forthright Building Society.

As instructed, Matthew then turned back to page 2 on the inside of the form. Panel 8 deals with joint ownership. It asks you to state whether or not the survivor can give a valid receipt for the proceeds of sale of the property. You should insert "yes" in the box if you have agreed to hold the property as joint tenants or "no" if you have agreed to hold the property as tenants in common. Panel 8 did not apply in Matthew's case.

Panel 9 is for use where a limited company is buying property or lending money on mortgage. Panel 10 applies where a mortgage is finally paid off. Neither were applicable here.

Panel 11 contains a list of reminders to ensure that the application is in order.

Finally panel 12 has a space for filling in the amount of the Land Registry fee and signing the form. Hodgson, Green & Co would sign the form and send it off to the Land Registry with their cheque for the fees, after completion and after they had attended to the stamping of the transfer.

It is important to deliver the application before the priority period conferred by the official search certificate expires. Building society solicitors can be slow in sending form A4 and the documents to the Land Registry for registration, so ask your building society's solicitor, at completion, not to delay in sending off the application even if this means not waiting for form 53 to arrive. That can be forwarded later.

A buyer without a mortgage has to attend to these matters himself. After completion, you should deliver the particulars of the transaction to the Inland Revenue and get your transfer stamped, if necessary, and send form A4 and the documents (land certificate or charge certificate with form 53, and transfer) to the Land Registry to arrive within your priority period.

preparing form Stamps L(A) 451

A buyer of freehold or leasehold land has to pay stamp duty where the purchase price of that property is more than £30,000. The deed transferring the property (in our case the transfer) has to be produced to the Inland Revenue, together with a statement of particulars about the instrument, within 30 days of its execution (completion). The transfer is then impressed with two stamps; one showing the amount of duty paid and the other (a PD stamp, the initials standing for 'particulars delivered') showing that the transfer has been produced to the Inland Revenue. A fine is payable for non-compliance and the Land Registry will not register a new owner unless the transfer to him has been duly stamped.

If no stamp duty is payable by the buyer (because the price is £30,000 or under) the transfer does not have to be produced to the Inland Revenue. However a statement of particulars about it must still be completed, and it must be sent along with the other documents to the Land Registry with the application for registration on A4 (or A5 if dealing with a part only). The Land Registry will then pass the statement of particulars to the Inland Revenue.

So, whether you have to pay stamp duty or not, you must give a statement of particulars about the transfer directly or indirectly to the Inland Revenue. The simplest and now universal method of supplying these particulars is to use form Stamps L(A) 451, commonly known as a PD form.

The form is headed *Particulars of instruments transferring or leasing land* and is divided into panels. In panel 1 (description of instrument), write: *transfer*. The date of instrument (panel 2) should be left blank until completion. Panels 3 and 4 call for the names and addresses of the transferor or lessor and transferee or lessee. In here should be written the names and addresses of the seller and the buyer; in Matthew's case, Mr and Mrs Timms and himself.

In panel 5 the "situation of the land" must be stated. Matthew simply wrote *14 Twintree Avenue, Minford, Surrey*. The rating authority is also asked for: in his case Minford D.C. Panel 6 requires details of the estate or interest transferred. Matthew wrote *freehold*. Had he been buying a leasehold house he would have stated "Remainder of ____ years lease from (date, namely the beginning of the term granted by the lease, not the date of the lease), at the rent of £____ per annum".

Panel 7 asks for the 'consideration' and gives a list [(a)–(f)] of alternative forms of payment; (a) will apply to most buyers, who will pay money for their house. Against capital payment in 7(a) Matthew wrote *£46,000*. Panels 8 and 9 will not normally be applicable; they relate to the creation of new mineral or sporting rights, restrictive covenants and so on. Matthew put *nil* in both panels. Hodgson, Green & Co would be attending to stamping the transfer on his behalf after completion. He wrote their name and address in panel 12, asking for the "name and address of signatory if other than transferee or lessee". Panel 11 requires details of the transferor's or lessor's solicitor. In here he put the name and address of Dodds & Son.

Form Stamps L(A) 451 is available from any Inland Revenue stamp office (address in the telephone directory) or by post from the Controller of Stamps Office, South West Wing, Bush House, Strand, London WC2B 4QN.

before completion

On wednesday 5 March, Matthew's official search certificate on form 94A arrived back from the Land Registry with its reassuring message: "Since the 10th day of January 1986 NO ADVERSE ENTRY HAS BEEN MADE THEREON". This meant that there has been no change in the register since the office copies that Dodds & Son had sent him were issued. The certificate was dated 6 February 1986 and under this date it said "Priority expires 22nd April 1986". This was the thirtieth working day (allowing for Easter) after the date of the issue of the certificate.

It may reassure the buyer to know that most solicitors in many years of practice will have never had a Land Registry search form returned with any adverse entry noted on it; the chances are very rare. If you are one of the unlucky ones and your search form is returned with particulars of an entry on the register since the date of your office copy entries and such an entry is a second mortgage, it can be dealt with in the same way as if it had happened on the office copies. Form 53 or the receipted mortgage deed should be handed over to you on completion, or an undertaking given to discharge the mortgage on completion and forward form 53 or the receipted deed within so-many days. If the entry relates to anything else, do not go ahead with the transaction without consulting a solicitor.

Also on 5 March, Matthew telephoned his bank manager and (having made the necessary arrangements previously) ordered a banker's draft for £10,231.75 payable to Dodds & Son.

you must get vacant possession

He also telephoned Flint & Morgan to check that Mr and Mrs Timms had made the necessary arrangements with them to inspect the property on the morning of completion. The importance of a buyer doing this (or having someone do it on his behalf) cannot be overstressed. Vacant possession must be given on completion. Getting rid of squatters, tenants or other persons in occupation can be a lengthy process. If you find someone living there who refuses to go, do not complete.

If a buyer cannot get vacant possession, he should immediately notify the seller's solicitor: it is, in the first place, the seller's problem because he has contracted to give vacant possession on completion. The buyer should also, as a matter of courtesy, inform his bank and the building society's solicitor of what is happening. And he will need to obtain the help of a solicitor if vacant possession is not given within a reasonable time.

STAGE III – COMPLETION

Friday 7 March 1986 was hectic for the Seatons, and was made more so by Matthew having to detach himself from the general operation and attend to his completion. He put together the documents he would need: the official certificate of search (form 94A), Land Registry application (Form A4), form Stamps L(A) 451, and the mortgage deed bearing the 'declaration and request' signed by Emma.

completion day

He went first to his bank in Hastings to collect the banker's draft in favour of Dodds & Son for £10,231.75, and then straight on to Minford. He met Mr Morgan, the estate agent, outside 14 Twintree Avenue, and together they inspected the house and garden thoroughly. No, there were no signs of anyone living there. The time was fast approaching 12 noon so he bade farewell to Mr Morgan and proceeded to 88 Great Winchester Street.

Inside, he was shown into an office where the three lots of solicitors (of Anderson, James & Pringle, of Dodds & Son and of Hodgson, Green & Co) awaited him, ready to get down to business.

the charge certificate

After brief introductions, Anderson, James & Pringle produced the charge certificate, which was handed to Matthew via Dodds & Son. He checked to see that it was the same as the office copies he was sent at the outset. If you were sent a photocopy of the land certificate or charge certificate (not an office copy), you should also see that the date stamped on the inside cover of the land or charge certificate is the same date as you were given, and quoted on your official search form. Matthew passed the charge certificate to Hodgson, Green & Co, who also examined it. With the charge certificate were some old documents – local search certificates, enquiries and requisitions – collected from when the property had changed hands before.

form 53 or an undertaking

Next Anderson, James & Pringle produced an undertaking regarding form 53 which, on request, they had addressed to Hodgson, Green & Co. It read as follows:

> ANDERSON, JAMES & PRINGLE
> *Solicitors* *88 Great Winchester Street*
> *Minford, Surrey*
>
> 7 March 1986
>
> To: Messrs Hodgson, Green & Co
>
> Dear Sirs,
>
> Re: 14 Twintree Avenue, Minford
>
> As solicitors for the Minford Building Society, we hereby undertake to forward you Form 53 executed by the society within 14 days.
>
> Yours faithfully,
> Anderson, James & Pringle

Another way of dealing with this matter is for the seller's solicitors to provide the undertaking, on the basis that it is the seller's responsibility to see that his mortgage is properly paid off and evidence of the paying off given to the purchaser. The form of undertaking would be like this:

> "In consideration of your today completing the purchase of 14 Twintree Avenue, Minford, we hereby undertake forthwith to pay over to the Minford Building Society the money required to redeem the mortgage dated 1st November 1971 and to forward form 53 to you as soon as it is received by us from the Minford Building Society. Dodds & Son"

Whichever form of undertaking is used, the building society's solicitor (or seller's solicitor, as the case may be), should ideally state that he has the mortgagee's authority to receive the money required to redeem the mortgage. In the improbable event of that solicitor absconding with the money, the building society and not the buyer, bears the loss.

the transfer

Dodds & Son then handed Matthew the transfer. He checked that this was the same document he had filled in and that it had been signed by Mr and Mrs Timms in the presence of a witness. Although not strictly necessary, the witness should add his address. It was agreed that Dodds & Son should date the transfer "7 March 1986". Matthew transcribed these details onto his copy of the transfer, so that he had a complete copy. This done, he handed the transfer to Hodgson, Green & Co.

the mortgage deed

Matthew now produced and signed the mortgage deed in the presence of the solicitor from Hodgson, Green & Co, who (after checking that the 'declaration and request' had been signed by Emma) countersigned as witness. The deed was again dated "7 March 1986". The date when the first monthly payment was to be made was also inserted into the deed. Matthew put these details into his copy of the mortgage deed so that he had a complete copy of that document, too. The actual deed was then taken by Hodgson, Green & Co.

Matthew handed to Hodgson, Green & Co his Land Registry application form (form A4), the form Stamps L(A) 451 and the official certificate of search (form 94A) showing a clear search.

Dodds & Son produced receipts for the current general rate, water rate and sewerage charge. Matthew checked them and handed them back. Finally they handed Matthew the keys to 14 Twintree Avenue.

now for the money

Matthew handed his banker's draft for £10,231.75 to Dodds & Son. Hodgson, Green & Co then handed two banker's drafts to Matthew. This was the correct procedure, as they (on behalf of the Forthright Building Society) were doing business only with Matthew and with no one else present. Matthew examined the drafts and saw that they had been made out as requested; one for £7,738.08 payable to the Minford Building Society and the other for £23,430.17 payable to Dodds & Son. He handed both to Dodds

& Son: he had no direct relationship with Minford Building Society. Dodds & Son checked both drafts and handed the one for £7,738.08 to Anderson, James & Pringle.

Completion was over.

delay in completion

Time is not 'of the essence' as far as the completion date is concerned, unless the special conditions of sale in the contract provide otherwise. In other words, it is not an essential term of the contract that the parties complete on the specified date and if they do not, neither party is entitled to treat the contracts as at an end. Nevertheless, failure to complete on the due date is a breach of contract, entitling the party not responsible for the delay to sue the other, the one who has caused the delay, for damages for any loss he has suffered as a consequence of the other's delay. The consequences of delay, especially in chain transactions, can be quite harsh and expensive. In addition, National condition 7 says that the buyer must pay the seller interest at 'the prescribed rate' on the balance of the purchase money for the period of delay, if the delay is due to the default of the buyer (of course any interest paid would be taken into account, that is deducted from the amount of damages, if the seller also sued the buyer for damages for breach of contract).

Law Society general condition 22 is a little more complicated. It gives the innocent party a choice of either suing the party responsible for the delay for ordinary damages, or taking instead interest at the 'contract rate' on the balance of the purchase money for the period of delay.

If there is delay either party can serve a 'special notice to complete'. You do this by simply writing a letter quoting the date of the contract and saying "I give you special notice to complete" and then referring to the condition under which the notice is served (Law Society general condition 23 or National condition 22). Once served, time becomes of the essence. A notice is deemed to have been 'served' if sent by registered post or recorded delivery (first class post, under the Law Society general condition 23) and not returned to the sender.

Under Law Society general condition 23(3) the party in default then has 15 working days to complete the contract; under 22(2) of the National conditions, 16 working days. If the buyer fails to comply with the notice, the seller can forfeit (that is, keep) the deposit and claim damages for any loss suffered on the re-sale. If the seller fails to comply, the buyer can recover his deposit and claim damages for any loss suffered.

If there is any default under the contract beyond a few days and it becomes necessary to serve a 'notice to complete', you would be well advised to consult a solicitor.

STAGE IV – AFTER COMPLETION

Matthew had no more legal formalities to attend to after completion, but this would not necessarily have been the case had he been buying a leasehold house. The buyer must usually notify the landlord's solicitor that the lease has been transferred to him.

Some leases demand that the transfer itself should be produced to the landlord's solicitor for inspection and return. Even if it does, the buyer need only send a copy. If the lease requires no more than that the landlord should be notified of the change of ownership, the buyer merely has to write a letter to the landlord's solicitor saying: "The property known as .... comprised in the lease dated .... for a term of ...... years was transferred on .... to ...." with the correct details.

It is usual to send the notification in duplicate, getting the landlord's solicitor to sign an acknowledgment on the copy and send it back as proof of the notification.

if buying without a mortgage

The formalities that remained in connection with Matthew's purchase would be dealt with by Hodgson, Green & Co. If you are buying without a mortgage, you will have to attend to these formalities yourself. If the purchase price of your house was over £30,000, the transfer must be stamped within 30 days. Stamping can be done in person at one of the Inland Revenue Stamp offices (look under Inland Revenue in the telephone book). All you have to do is take your completed form Stamps L(A) 451 with you. The clerk or enquiry department at the stamp office will assist you, if necessary.

It is possible to send deeds for stamping through the post, using form Stamps 61 (available from head post offices) which has to be completed and sent to The Controller of Stamps, Inland Revenue (D) (Direct Post Section), West Bank, Barrington Road, Worthing, West Sussex, with the transfer and payment for the correct amount of stamp duty.

Then you must send the land certificate, or charge certificate together with form 53, and the transfer to the Land Registry, together with your application on form A4 to be registered as the new proprietor and a cheque for the Land Registry fees. There is no need to send the official certificate of search on Form 94A because the original records are with the Land Registry anyway.

If no stamp duty is payable on your purchase (because you paid £30,000 or less), you do not have to get the transfer stamped. You simply send the documents described above together with your application for registration *and form Stamps L(A) 451* to the Land Registry. They will then pass form Stamps L(A) 451 on to the Inland Revenue.

In either case, remember to lodge your application with the Land Registry before your priority period expires even if this means not waiting for form 53.

just to make sure

It takes anything from about three to eight or more working weeks for the registration to be completed. You can check that all is well by filling in form A44 and sending it to the appropriate district land registry. The office copy which the Land Registry send in response should show you as the new proprietor. No fee is payable for this service.

Emma's rights of occupation

Under the Matrimonial Homes Act 1983 a spouse (husband or wife) has certain rights of occupation (that is, rights to live there) in the matrimonial home, owned by the other spouse. The rights are:

- if living in the home, a right not to be evicted or excluded from the home by the owner-spouse; or
- if not living in the home, a right to live there under an order of the court.

These rights are in addition to any interest he or she may have in the property by virtue of contributions made to the purchase price or subsequent improvements to the property.

registration of a matrimonial notice

The rights of occupation can be protected, in the case of registered property, by registration of a notice.

This is done on form 99 and a fee of £5 is payable. The land certificate does not have to be produced to the registrar to register this type of notice, and the consent of the owner-spouse is therefore not necessary (where the home is subject to a mortgage, the Land Registry will already have the land certificate anyway, the building society or other lender being issued with a charge certificate). You do, however, need the title number of the home to make the application on form 99. If you are reluctant to ask your husband or wife for this (or he or she will not tell you) you can find it out by making an application for an *Official Search of the Index Map* on form 96. All you need do is put the address of the home on the form, sign and date it, and send it to the Land Registry. The Land Registry will tell you the title number in the *Certificate of Result of Official Search* which is sent back to you. If there is any other information on the certificate of result, you can ignore it for this purpose. No fee is payable for a search of the index map.

The effect of registering a notice on form 99 is that all dealings with the home take effect subject to the interest that is protected, unless the non-owner spouse agrees to the notice being cancelled. In other words, a husband cannot sell or mortgage the property over his wife's head (and vice versa). The owner-spouse will not be informed of the registration – the aim, supposedly, being to protect a spouse against an angry husband or wife.

Protection of a spouse's rights of occupation in the matrimonial home belonging to the other spouse by registration is usually described as a 'hostile registration', presumably because it implies lack of trust by one spouse in the other. This type of registration is perhaps rarer than it should be: usually it is not until a marriage goes wrong that the parties begin to think about their individual rights.

Emma, being a far-sighted and cautious woman decided that she would apply for the registration of a notice against 14 Twintree Avenue on form 99 – just in case their marriage should take a turn for the worse.

At the top of the form she wrote the name and address of Tunbridge Wells District Land Registry; this was where she would send her application. In the box underneath she filled in – *Minford, Surrey*, the title number – *SY43271604*; and the property – *14 Twintree Avenue, Minford, Surrey*. She filled in clause 1, stating that she was applying to protect her rights of occupation in the property by the registration of a notice, and clause 2, stating that she was the wife of Matthew John Seaton, the registered proprietor. Clauses 3 and 4 were inapplicable, so she crossed them out; 3 only applies where the court has made an order regarding the rights of occupation; 4, where there is already a subsisting registration. She then signed and dated the form and sent it to Tunbridge Wells District Land Registry with a cheque for £5. Since she did not own the house jointly with Matthew, this was a sensible way of ensuring that he could not sell or mortgage the house without her knowing.

some costs and charges connected with the legal side of buying a house

official fees

price of house	*Land Registry fee on dealing*	*stamp duty*
£20,000	£ 40.00	—
30,000	65.00	—
30,100	70.00	£301.00
35,000	80.00	350.00
40,000	90.00	400.00
50,000	120.00	500.00

building society

amount of loan	*solicitor's fee for d-i-y conveyancer*	
	repayment mortgage	*endowment mortgage*
£10,000	£ 78.75	£ 91.88
15,000	93.75	109.38
20,000	101.25	118.13
25,000	108.75	126.88
35,000	114.38	133.44

surveyor's charges

price of house	*valuation for mortgage*	*'middle' structural report*
£10,000	£30.00	£115.00
20,000	47.00	125.00
30,000	59.00	135.00
40,000	65.00	150.00
50,000	70.00	160.00

notes

Land Registry fees on 'dealing', that is when a house is sold to a new proprietor, are laid down in the current Land Registry Fee Order (S.I. 1985/359 available from HMSO, price £2.25). At present, the fee starts at £10 where the purchase price is between £4,000 and £10,000 and then goes up by £5 per £2,000 of the price.

stamp duty is laid down in the apprioriate Finance Act and at present is nil up to a purchase price of £30,000, and 1 per cent of the price of a house costing more than £30,000.

building society solicitor's fee is based on the amount of the loan, not the purchase price of the house. The fee must be 'fair and reasonable' and there is a scale of charges recommended by the Building Societies Association where the solicitor is acting for the lender only. Where the same solicitor acts for the buyer and his lender, the guideline charges are recommended jointly by the Building Societies Association and the Law Society.

surveyors' fees for a valuation report to the building society vary from one building society to another. The fees given here are a very rough indication only, as are those for a surveyor's 'middle' report on the state of repair and condition of a property. For a full structural survey, the buyer should negotiate a fee.

up to date forms

The dates on the forms you may buy from Oyez Stationery are indicated by the month (from 1 for January to 12 for December) followed by the last two digits of the year.

In February 1986 the current edition dates of the forms are as follows:

Conveyancing 29 (Long) 4-85
Con 29 (Supplementary) 1-85
Con.29A 11-85
Con.29D 1-86
Form LLC1 3-85
Conveyancing 28B 9-85
Form 18 8-84
Form 19(JP) 11-85
Form 94A 12-85
Form K16 10-85
Form A4 8-84
Form A44 7-85
Form 201 12-82
Conveyancing 46A 3-84

SELLING

What follows will tell you how to do the conveyancing involved when you sell your house. As in the case of buying, the instructions are limited to the sale of a house which is not newly-built and which is already registered at the Land Registry with freehold or leasehold title absolute, which is not let to tenants and will be sold with vacant possession. Selling is really the mirror image of buying. To avoid repetition, it is assumed in what follows that the reader has become familiar with the process of buying – or at least has followed it by reading the description of what Matthew Seaton did when buying his house.

the forms you will need

1 print of *Application for Office Copies* (A44).
3 prints of EITHER The Law Society's Contract for Sale (1984 Revision) OR The National Contract of Sale (Twentieth Edition) (with special conditions).
1 print of *Authority to inspect the register* (Form 201).
1 print of *Notice of Sale of property and request for apportionments of rates* (Conveyancing 46A).

All these forms can be bought from Oyez shops or by post from Oyez Stationery (see pages 29 and 30).

when you have found a buyer

The first step in any sale is to find a buyer. The book *Which? way to buy, sell and move house* gives detailed information on the various methods of how to set about this.

Let us assume that you have reached the stage where you have decided to sell your house, either independently or simultaneously with your purchase of another house. You have agreed a price and got the name and address of your buyer and his solicitor.

preliminary deposit

Your buyer might have paid a small preliminary deposit to your estate agents, which they will hold as stakeholders. Accepting a preliminary deposit does not constitute a binding agreement that the house is not to be shown or offered to anyone else. If you are selling privately, the buyer may offer you such a deposit. If you accept his money, give him a written receipt but make sure that the receipt, and any other writing you give or send to him or his solicitors at this stage, contains the words "subject to contract". This will prevent a binding contract coming into force until you are ready. Remember that a binding obligation to sell arises only on exchange of contracts.

deeds and documents

The next stage in the sale is the preparation of the draft contract. For this you need the deeds of the property, which in the case of registered land are the land certificate or the charge certificate.

Where there is no mortgage on the property, the land certificate will either be in your possession or deposited with your bank for safe keeping, or with the solicitor who acted for you on your purchase. You will probably be required to sign a receipt when you get it back.

If there is an existing mortgage, the charge certificate will be held by the building society or other lender. They will not give you the charge certificate: it represents the security for the loan, and they will insist on keeping it until they are repaid in full. Anyway, all you really need at this stage is the registered title number of the property so that you can obtain office copies of the entries on the register and filed plan from the Land Registry. Ask your lender to let you know the title number.

If you had a solicitor when you bought your house, ask him for all the old papers. These may be useful to you later when you have to deal with your buyer's enquiries about the property. Provided that all his fees have been paid, you are entitled to be sent all your documents in your solicitor's file, except notes prepared by the solicitor for his own benefit and letters written to him by you. But, strictly speaking, solicitors need only keep papers for six years.

getting office copies

Any copy document which has to be sent to the buyer's solicitor with the draft contract should be (and where the Law Society's Contract for Sale is used it must be) an 'office copy'. It is a Law Society recommendation and is the current practice amongst seller's solicitors to send a complete set of office copy entries to the other side at this stage. So even if you have the land certificate in your possession, you should obtain office copies of the entries on the register and the filed plan. (They would also show if anyone has entered any charges affecting the property or your right to sell it.)

The form for applying for these is form A44, called *Application for Office Copies*. Only you or someone with your permission may apply for office copies, so you must fill in your name and address and put a cross in the square at the top of the form declaring: "I am/We are the registered proprietor". Fill in the title number, the county and district, a short description of the property (the postal address is usually sufficient) and your full name. It is a good idea to ask for two copies of the entries on the register and filed plan, so that you will always have one copy on your file for reference throughout the conveyancing transaction. Write "2" next to boxes C and D. If you need office copies of any documents referred to on the register and filed at the Land Registry, you should state which documents you need after box F. Such a document might be one which creates a restrictive covenant the benefit of which the property enjoys, or a lease, if the property is leasehold. Box E only applies where part only of a large registered estate is being sold off, for example where you own a couple of adjoining cottages and are selling one of them. The next two panels are inapplicable.

Sign and date the form and send it to the district land registry which covers the district your property is in. The office copies will be sent to you by post after a few days. No fee is payable for obtaining office copies.

A seller who is really anxious to get things moving can also apply for a local land charges search certificate (on form LLC1) and replies to enquiries of the local authority (on form Con.29A) or D) in advance. The result of such a search is transferable, so the buyer will be able to use it. In areas where there is a considerable delay in getting a reply from the local authority, this can be a useful step. (But it may become out of date if there is delay in finding a buyer or in the contract proceedings, in which case the buyer will have to carry out another search.)

the draft contract

Most solicitors in England and Wales use printed forms of contract incorporating either the Law Society's general conditions of sale (1984 revision) or the National conditions of sale (20th Edition). These can be bought from Oyez or other law stationers. The choice of contract form is yours; if you decide to use the National contract form, you should buy the one with special conditions on the back.

You will need to complete three copies of the contract form; two are sent to the buyer's solicitor for approval, one of which will be returned to you to exchange later with the buyer. You will then be able to tell that there have been no alterations made without your knowledge by checking against the copy you retained.

Here we have filled in the Law Society's and National form of contract on the assumption that Michael Basset has agreed (through Flint & Morgan, estate agents) to sell 22 Twintree Avenue to Iris Porter for £49,000, subject to contract. Michael has further agreed to sell the fitted carpets separately to Miss Porter for the sum of £500. Miss Porter's solicitors are Meade, Brown & Co of 6 Green Street, Minford, Surrey. A provisional completion date of 24 July 1986 suits both parties.

A detailed explanation of how to complete both standard forms of contract appears at pages 31 to 45. Here are some points to remember about the draft contract form.

the deposit

Both sets of standard conditions state that on exchange of contracts the buyer shall pay a deposit of ten per cent of the purchase price to the seller's solicitors as stakeholders. Naturally this is impossible where the seller is doing his own conveyancing. Michael is selling through a firm of estate agents, Flint & Morgan.

IMPORTANT
This is a technical document, designed to create specific legal rights and obligations. It is recommended for use only in accordance with the advice of your solicitors.

THE LAW SOCIETY'S CONTRACT FOR SALE (1984 REVISION)

AGREEMENT made the day of 1986

BETWEEN MICHAEL BASSET of 22 Twintree Avenue, Minford, Surrey — Vendor

and IRIS PORTER of 7 Chapel Street, Minford, Surrey — Purchaser

IT is agreed that the Vendor shall sell and the Purchaser shall purchase in accordance with the following special conditions the property described in the particulars below at the price of

PARTICULARS—ALL THAT freehold/~~leasehold~~ property known as 22 Twintree Avenue, Minford, Surrey

SPECIAL CONDITIONS OF SALE—SEE BACK PAGE

Purchase money	49,000	00
less deposit paid	4,900	00
	44,100	00
Chattels, fittings etc.	500	00
Balance	44,600	00

SIGNED

Vendor/Purchaser

Vendor's Solicitors — Ref.

Purchaser's Solicitors Meade, Brown & Co., 6 Green Street, Minford, Surrey — Ref.

Local Authorities Minford District Council, Surrey County Council

SPECIAL CONDITIONS

A. The property is sold subject to The Law Society's General Conditions of Sale (1984 Revision) ("general conditions") printed within so far as they are not varied by or inconsistent with these special conditions but general condition 8(5) shall apply in any event.

B. For the purposes of the following general conditions—

1(*b*)	the contract rate is 3 % per annum above the base rate from time to time of Lloyds Bank p.l.c.
1(c)	contractual completion date is 198
21(2)(*b*)	the specified bank is
21(5)(a)	the latest time is 2 ~~am~~/pm
1(g)	the following are not working days
5(3)	the retained land is

C. General condition 4 shall not apply. [~~For the purposes of general condition 4(2) the period shall be from the date hereof and for the purposes of general condition 4(3)(b) the specified use is~~]

D. The Vendor shall convey as Beneficial Owner

E. The Vendor's title is registered with absolute title under Title No. SY52309514 in the Tunbridge Wells District Land Registry.
The Vendor authorises the Purchaser's solicitors to inspect the register and to obtain office copies thereof.

~~(or) E. The abstract of title shall begin with~~

F. The property is sold with vacant possession on completion.

(or) ~~F. The property is sold subject to the following leases or tenancies~~

G. The property is sold subject to the restrictions and stipulations referred to in Entry number 1 on the charges register of the abovementioned title number SY52309514, so far as they are subsisting and capable of being enforced or of taking effect. A copy of the said restrictions and stipulations having been supplied to the purchaser he shall be deemed to purchase with full knowledge thereof and shall raise no requisition or enquiry thereon

H. The deposit is to be paid to Flint & Morgan of 43 High Street, Minford, Surrey (estate agents) and is to be held by them as stakeholders

I. The Vendor agrees to sell and the Purchaser agrees to buy the fitted carpets at present on the property for the sum of £500.00 payable on completion

Re: 22 Twintree Avenue, Minford, Surrey   Basset   to   Porter

SPECIAL CONDITIONS OF SALE

A. Condition 3 of the National Conditions of Sale shall (not) have effect [~~But it shall not apply to a matter or matters affecting the value of the property by less than £ or to the following:—~~

B. Title shall be deduced and shall commence as follows:—
The Vendor's title shall be deduced in accordance with section 110 of the Land Registration Act 1925

C. The sale is with vacant possession/~~subject to the existing tenancy of which details have been supplied to the Purchaser/subject to the following tenancies:—~~

D. The property is sold on the footing that the authorised use thereof for the purposes of the Planning Acts is the use (if any) specified in the particulars of sale/use as
private dwelling house

E. The sale includes the chattels fittings and separate items specified ~~in the inventory annexed~~ below which are to be taken by the Purchaser for a sum (additional to the purchase price of the property) of £500.00/ ~~to be ascertained by a valuation to be made by at the expense of~~
Fitted Carpets at present in the property

F. The property is sold subject so far as they are subsisting and capable of being enforced or of taking effect to the restrictions and stipulations referred to in Entry 1 on the charges register of the abovementioned title number SY52309514. A copy of the said restrictions and stipulations having been supplied to the purchaser he shall be deemed to purchase with full knowledge thereof and shall raise no requisition or enquiry thereon

G. The deposit shall be paid to Flint & Morgan of 43 High Street, Minford, Surrey (estate agents) and is to be held by them as stakeholders

CONTRACT OF SALE

The National Conditions of Sale, Twentieth Edition

Vendor MICHAEL BASSET of 22 Twintree Avenue, Minford, Surrey

Purchaser IRIS PORTER of 7 Chapel Street, Minford, Surrey

Registered Land			
District Land Registry: Tunbridge Wells	Purchase price	£ 49,000	00
	Deposit	£ 4,900	00
Title Number: SY 523 09514	Balance payable	£ 44,100	00
Agreed rate of interest: 3% per annum above the base rate from time to time of Lloyds Bank p.l.c.	Price fixed for chattels or valuation money (if any)	£ 500	00
	Total	£ 44,600	00

Property and interest therein sold: freehold property known as 22 Twintree Avenue, Minford, Surrey

Vendor sells as Beneficial Owner   Completion date:

AGREED that the Vendor sells and the Purchaser buys as above, subject to the Special Conditions endorsed hereon and to the National Conditions of Sale Twentieth Edition so far as the latter Conditions are not inconsistent with the Special Conditions.

* Signed

Date   19

* This is a form of legal document. Neither the form nor the National Conditions of Sale which the form embodies, were produced or drafted for use, without technical assistance, by persons unfamiliar with the law and practice of conveyancing.

The special conditions of his draft contract therefore provide for the deposit to be paid to them as stakeholders. If you are not selling through agents, you can suggest to the buyer that you open a joint account at a bank, by using the following special condition in the contract:

> 'A deposit of 10 per cent of the purchase price is to be paid by the buyer on exchange of contracts and shall be held in a joint account to be opened in the name of the seller and of the buyer or his solicitors at (*name and address of bank*). Cheques drawn on the account must be signed by both parties.'

Your own bank or the buyer's solicitor's bank would be appropriate. The account could be in the joint names of the seller and buyer or the seller and the buyer's solicitor. The deposit is paid into this account by the buyer and stays there until the sale is completed. On completion, the buyer's solicitor hands over a cheque drawn on the joint account signed by the buyer or his solicitor. The seller then countersigns the cheque and presents it in the normal way. The joint account is then closed.

The payment of reduced deposits (that is less than 10 per cent) was discussed at p. 32/33. Where the Law Society's contract form is used, no special condition is needed to cover this. The seller is protected if it later looks like the buyer is going to back out of the sale. General condition 9 says that if the seller has to serve a notice to complete (because of the buyer's delay in completing) the buyer must pay him the balance of the ten per cent deposit. This ensures that if the sale does fall through, through no fault of his own, the seller can get and keep ('forfeit') the full deposit.

Reduced deposits are not catered for in the National condition. If you decide to accept one, you need to provide, by way of special condition, first for the payment of the reduced deposit and second for a sum equivalent to a full 10 per cent deposit being forfeited. The following special condition might be written into the contract:

> "A deposit of __ per cent of the purchase price is to be paid by the buyer on exchange of contracts. Upon service by the seller of a completion notice, the buyer shall pay to the seller the difference between a deposit of 10 per cent of the purchase price and the sum he has actually paid."

restrictive covenants

Details of the restrictive covenant entries on the charges register can be found in your office copies. There is no need to refer to any mortgage you may have taken out on the security of the property, because it will have to be discharged on completion and you do not sell subject to it. Your office copies will also help you fill in details of the title number and district land registry, required by both contract forms.

leaseholds

Where the property is leasehold, you have to send a copy of the lease to the buyer's solicitor with the draft contract. If the property is not subject to a mortgage, you will probably have the lease with the land certificate. If it is subject to a mortgage, the building society or other lender will hold the lease, but will provide you with a copy of it (if you do not have one already), possibly on payment of a small charge. The particulars of the lease that have to be given in the draft contract will appear in the lease itself.

joint owners

Remember that where joint owners are selling, both must be a party to the contract and it is preferable for them to contract to convey as 'trustees for sale' rather than as 'beneficial owners' (see also page 38/39).

do not let the buyer in too soon

It is usual to leave the completion date blank in the draft contract, to be filled in on exchange of contracts. All being well, 24 July 1986 would be put in Michael Basset's.

Sometimes a buyer is anxious to take possession of the property as quickly as possible. But it would be foolish to let a buyer into occupation before contracts are exchanged. And even if a buyer has signed a binding contract, he should not be allowed to go into occupation before completion: it might encourage him to delay it. Furthermore, a seller might have difficulties in regaining possession of a house from a buyer who was allowed in before completion, and who then refuses, or is unable, to complete his purchase.

Under both the Law Society general and the National conditions, if a buyer is let into occupation before completion, he occupies as a 'licensee' not as a 'tenant'. This excludes any protection conferred by the Rent Act 1977 (as amended). He must pay all outgoings – ground rent, general rate, water rate, sewerage charge and insurance – and also interest on the balance of the purchase price at the 'contract' or 'prescribed' rate (Law Society general condition 18; National condition 8).

procedure

When you have completed the copies of either the Law Society or National contract for sale, send two copies to the buyer's solicitor, together with the office copies of the entries on the register and the filed plan. When he returns it to you, check against the copy you have retained to see if there have been any amendments made and, if so, that they are acceptable. When the draft contract has been approved (with or without amendments) he will send you back one copy which you will eventually use to exchange with the buyer. At this stage, neither copy should be signed or dated. In the covering letter you write to the buyer's solicitor, do not forget to incorporate the words 'subject to contract'.

Although not technically necessary until after exchange of contracts, it is a good idea to send office copies of the entries on the register and the filed plan to the buyer's solicitor with the draft contract. It saves time and trouble later, and if by any chance you have misunderstood some aspect of the matter, or inaccurately transposed the information given in the register in filling in the draft contract, any such errors will be evident to the buyer's solicitor before contracts are exchanged; he cannot then later complain that he was misled by the way in which the contract was worded. If you bought your house before 1976 and you do not wish your buyer to know the price you paid for it, cut out the figure in the office copy of the proprietorship register before you send it off.

enquiries before contract

After the buyer's solicitor has received the draft contract, he will send you his preliminary enquiries, probably on form Conveyancing 29 (Long) accompanied, if his client is a first-time buyer, by supplementary enquiries on form Con.29 (Supplementary). The extent of the seller's duty of disclosure of matters relevant to the property is discussed at pages 57/58, and an explanation of the meaning and relevance of the printed form enquiries on pages 73 to 80.

Try and be as helpful and informative as you can in answering the questions put to you, but remember that if you say something about the property which turns out to be untrue after exchange of contracts, it may amount to a misrepresentation entitling the buyer to rescind the contract (end it) and/or claim damages. If you have got back your old file from the solicitor who acted when you bought your house, you may find the preliminary enquiries then asked, and the replies then given. These may help you to reply to the present enquiries.

If there are any questions you cannot understand, ask the buyer's solicitor to explain them to you.

Question 7(B) on form Conveyancing 29 (Long) will ask if there is anyone living in the property who is not a party to the sale and, if so, the nature of his or her interest if any. If your wife/husband or anyone else who is not a registered proprietor is living with you, they will have to sign the contract to show that they agree to the sale.

in the interim

After you have sent back the replies to the enquiries before contract, there is likely to be a lull in the transaction. The buyer now makes his local land charges search and enquiries of the local authority, has the house surveyed, arranges insurance and, if necessary, waits for his mortgage offer to come through.

During this period there may be some correspondence between you (remember to include the words "subject to contract") and the buyer's solicitor about the draft contract. He may accept it entirely or urge amendments. It is generally up to the seller to determine the terms on which he will sell. The buyer's solicitor may suggest the addition or alteration of one or two clauses in the special conditions to cover various points. But in the sale of a second-hand house with a registered freehold or leasehold title absolute, there should be little difficulty in agreeing the contract.

If the buyer encounters difficulty in getting his mortgage or in selling his house, there may well be delay and frustration at this stage. If this goes on, you will have to decide whether to continue with this sale or find another buyer.

Before preparing your engrossment of the contract, be quite sure that it is in the form both you and the buyer's solicitor have agreed. If no amendments or only very minor ones have been made, you can use as your engrossment the top copy of the draft contract which the buyer's solicitor has returned approved.

exchange of contracts

The contract for the sale of a house really consists of two separate identical documents, one of which is signed by the seller and the other by the buyer. It is the custom for the buyer's solicitor to send his client's signed contract to the seller first. This he will do when he has received back his local land charges search certificate and replies to his enquiries of the local authority and once the buyer has received a satisfactory survey report and, if necessary, mortgage offer (this is usually about five to six weeks after the buyer first offered to buy the property).

When you receive the buyer's part of the contract, check carefully that it is in the form you have agreed and that the buyer's signature (or signatures if there is more than one) is in the appropriate place on the front of the form. Also make sure that the buyer has paid the 10 per cent deposit (or such sum as has been agreed) to the estate agent or into the joint account. Where the contract incorporates the Law Society's general conditions of sale, the deposit should have been paid by banker's draft or solicitor's cheque. The National conditions do not specify the mode of payment of the deposit, but cash is really the only other acceptable alternative. If the buyer's own cheque has been sent for the deposit, wait until it has been cleared through the bank before doing anything further.

Up to this point, either you or your buyer can call the deal off, without giving any reason.

The contract signed by the buyer will be undated. Before sending your signed contract to the buyer's solicitor, date both contracts with the date of exchange. Also, fill in the completion date on both. This date is usually four weeks after exchange and you will probably have already agreed a completion date with your buyer. If no completion date is filled in, the fall-back conditions in the contract will apply: 26 working days after exchange of contracts under National condition 5, or 25 working days under Law Society general condition 21.

The contract becomes binding on you and the buyer the moment when you, having received the buyer's signed contract, post to the buyer's solicitor an identical contract signed by yourself (and if co-owners, your husband/wife or other person). Each party or his solicitor then holds a separate identical contract signed by the other and an exchange of contracts has been effected.

The buyer's solicitors may only be prepared to exchange contracts personally at their office, because otherwise they would not know the precise time contracts are exchanged, which may be very important if the buyer also has a property to sell contemporaneously.

what you must also send

You will already have sent office copies of the entries on the register (and any other filed documents) and the filed plan to the buyer's solicitor with the draft contract. (If by any chance you did not send the office copies with the draft contract, now is the time to do so.) All that remains outstanding for you to do, by way of proving your title to your house, is to supply him with an authority to inspect the register so that he can make his official search of the register (on form 94A or 94B) a week before completion. Special condition E on the Law Society's contract incorporates the seller's authority for the buyer's solicitors to inspect the register, in which case you need do nothing more than send him the signed contract. The National conditions do not incorporate such an authority. You will therefore have to send the buyer's solicitor, with the signed contract, a separate authority to inspect the register.

An authority to inspect the register can be done on form 201, obtainable from Oyez shops. It is small and easy to fill in and must be signed by you as registered proprietor (or by both you and your wife/husband or any other person, if you are joint proprietors). It should be worded so as to allow the buyer's solicitor to inspect the register.

A letter addressed to the Land Registry can be used instead of form 201:

22 Twintree Avenue
Minford, Surrey

24 June 1986

To: The Chief Land Registrar
Tunbridge Wells District Land Registry

Dear Sir,

Title No SY 52309514
22 Twintree Avenue, Minford, Surrey

Please permit Messrs Meade, Brown & Co, of 6 Green Street, Minford, Surrey who are solicitors acting for Iris Porter, a buyer, to inspect the register relating to the above title.

Yours faithfully,
Michael Basset
(Registered proprietor)

If your buyer is buying with the aid of a mortgage, you will be asked to provide an additional authority for the buyer's building society's (or other lender's) solicitors to inspect the register.

chain transactions

It happens fairly often that a person who is selling his home must make sure that he has another one to move to. Conversely, a buyer needs to be sure that he has sold his house before he buys another. In this way, a number of dependent transactions can be linked together to form a chain. Some fine timing is often necessary to resolve this situation. Simultaneous exchange of contracts by telephone is not a solution to this problem recommended to a person doing his own conveyancing.

Remember that if you are both buying a new house and selling your present one, you should not send off the signed contract for your purchase until you have received your buyer's signed contract for the house you are selling. Once you have received your signed contract of sale, a bridging loan might solve the problem of finding the deposit needed for your purchase. Another solution might be to persuade your buyer's solicitor to make the deposit payable to your seller's solicitor.

Even after exchange of contracts there might be difficulty in synchronising completion dates, in the case of interdependent sales and purchases. Again, your bank may be willing to give you temporary bridging finance to enable you to complete the purchase of your new home before you complete the sale of your present one. But the bank is likely only to be willing to do this after you have a binding contract of sale on your present home. The bank will probably also require a solicitor's undertaking to remit part or all of the sale money to them once the sale has been completed; the amount necessary to repay the loan, interest and arrangement fee. It should not be too difficult for you to persuade your buyer's solicitor to give your bank such an undertaking, although he will probably charge you a small fee for doing so. If you do manage to get a loan from the bank, make sure that when the loan is granted it is expressed in such terms as to be eligible for tax relief (an ordinary bank overdraft or personal loan is not).

preparing to pay off the mortgage

When you have exchanged contracts with a buyer, and are therefore in a position to assume that the sale will go through, you should contact your building society or other lender to let them know that you will shortly be wanting to pay off your outstanding mortgage. If you know your completion date, you can specify that as being the date on which you hope to be paying off the mortgage.

redemption charge

Some mortgages contain a clause saying that you must give three months' notice (or some other length of time) of your intention to pay off the loan. This means that you will have to pay interest on the outstanding loan (but not capital repayments) up to a day three months from the date on which you give official notice to the building society. This clause used to be very strictly enforced by building societies, but this is no longer so.

Some building societies require 'reasonable notice', for administrative purposes so that the necessary calculations can be made; ten days would be a reasonable period. With some building societies, the rules provide for additional interest to be charged on redemption within the first five years of the mortgage – but in practice they may work to a two years' period.

Some building societies waive the redemption charges for people who apply for another mortgage for the new house they are buying and banks tend not to make a charge for early redemption. If an early redemption charge is imposed, however, the sooner you give notice, the less you will have to pay by way of interest. If anything should happen to delay the sale of your house, you can withdraw your notice to the building society.

When you write to your lender, ask exactly how much money will be required to pay off the mortgage on the day fixed for completion. If there should be a delay to the completion date, there would need to be an adjustment in the amount the building society requires to pay off the mortgage. Many building societies, when notifying a mortgagor of the amount required to pay off the loan on a given date, also state the amount of interest that will accrue each day after that, so that the borrower does not have to go back to the building society for a recalculation if completion is slightly delayed. Some building societies, in fact, charge interest right up to the end of the month in which redemption is made, regardless of the actual date of the transaction.

Ask also whether the banker's draft for the amount to redeem the mortgage should be made payable to the building society itself, or to its solicitors.

You should also ask about the fees of the solicitors for the building society (or other lender) whose existing mortgage is paid off. These fees must be met by you the borrower. Not much legal work is involved in the redemption of a mortgage, and the fee will probably be in the region of £15 (there may also be a 'deeds handling fee' of about the same amount). You should agree the amount beforehand and will probably be asked to pay it at completion.

requisitions on title

Shortly after exchange of contracts, the buyer's solicitor will send you his requisitions on title, on form Conveyancing 28B. The meaning and relevance of the requisitions and the time limits for making and replying to them were considered at pages 106 to 108.

First, you will be asked to confirm that there has been no change to the answers you gave to the preliminary enquiries. If there has not, your reply should be: "The seller is not aware of any variation." If there has been any change (such as a new additional person in occupation, or mains water now put in, or change in rateable value, or receipt of a local authority notice), details should be given.

Secondly, you will be asked to produce at completion receipts for any outgoings you intend to apportion in your completion statement, and for that statement.

You need not answer 3(B), because recent office copies of the entries on the register and filed plan will have been sent by you to the buyer.

Question 4 states that all subsisting mortgages must be discharged on or before completion. You obviously confirm this.

Then it asks whether "a vacating receipt, discharge of registered charge or consent to dealing" will be handed over at completion. The 'discharge of registered charge' applies to the sale of a registered house within the scope of this book. The discharge will be on form 53 executed by your lender. Often a building society does not hand over form 53 at completion but an undertaking to do so. Question 4(B)(iii) therefore asks for the proposed terms of such an undertaking. A solicitor's undertaking is something special. Provided that it is not qualified in any way, it puts the solicitor under a personal obligation to carry out its terms, even if his client defaults. If a buyer and/or his building society is not going to be handed form 53 on completion, he or his solicitor will need to have your mortgagee's (building society's or other lender's) solicitor's personal and unqualified undertaking to forward form 53 to him within a specified period, usually 14 days. The building society's (or other lender's) solicitor might also be required to state that he has the society's (or other lender's) authority to accept the money required to redeem the mortgage on their behalf.

Requisition 5 states that vacant possession must be given on completion. This has already been stated in the contract, and you should write "agreed". It then asks if every person in occupation of the property has agreed to vacate it before or on completion. The answer to this question is important to a buyer: he must ensure that he will not be saddled with any occupational overriding interests once he becomes the registered proprietor of the house. The requisition then asks about keys; arrangements about these can be made later.

Question 7 asks for details regarding actual completion. You will probably not be able to supply these until a later date.

Then may follow extra questions relevant to your particular sale. For example, where your wife or husband is not a joint proprietor, she or he may have registered a notice, protecting her/his rights of occupation in the property under the Matrimonial Homes Act 1983. Such a notice would appear on the office copy entries, and you would be asked to confirm that you will hand over a form signed by your wife or husband stating she or he consents to the cancellation of the notice.

Sign and date the requisitions at the end of the form and send it back to the buyer's solicitor, keeping a copy for your file.

The requisitions on title may, instead of being on a printed form, be the buyer's solicitor's own home-made variety. If they present any problem or if you do not understand any of the questions, ask the buyer's solicitor to explain them.

the transfer

With his requisitions the buyer's solicitor usually sends the draft transfer for your approval, together with a copy for your use. The transfer will invariably be on form 19 *Transfer of whole* and will follow the lines of the transfer to Matthew Seaton on pages 109 to 112. This form is very simple and there is usually little room for amendments and you will be invited to treat the top copy as the engrossment, to be executed by you and handed over at completion.

You should check the details written on to the transfer form; provided they are correct you can approve it. All you need do is write to the buyer's solicitor saying that you approve the draft transfer. You keep the top copy for use as the engrossment, and should keep the carbon copy of the transfer for your file.

Where the transfer is to the buyers as joint proprietors, form 19 (JP) will be used. The transfer will contain a clause regulating the joint proprietors' rights between themselves, but this need not concern you. The only difference it will make is that you will have to return the top copy to the buyer's solicitor (if approved by you and thus treated as the engrossment) for execution by his clients. He will then return it for you to execute and hand over at completion.

buyer's building society (or other lender)

If a buyer is obtaining part of his purchase price on mortgage, he will have to deal with his building society's (or other mortgagee's) requisitions on title (see pages 116 to 119). Where the same solicitor is acting for the buyer and the lender he will usually incorporate the lender's requisitions into the requisitions on title he sends to the seller on Conveyancing 28B, so killing two birds with one stone.

Where different solicitors act for the lender and the buyer, you may find that you get another set of requisitions to answer, put by the lender's solicitor. The buyer's solicitor may say: "Our client's mortgagees have raised the following requisitions in addition to those which you have already answered and we shall be glad if you will let us have replies".

These requisitions may technically be out of time. Under the Law Society's general conditions, requisitions must be made within 6 working days of delivery of the seller's title (the office copies and authority to inspect the register) or of the date of the contract, whichever is the later; under the National conditions the buyer has 11 working days from delivery of the seller's title to make his requisitions. Technically you are entitled to refuse to answer requisitions that are made out of time, but it would be highly unusual to refuse to answer these additional questions on this ground.

The lender's requisitions will probably be similar to those you have already answered and should not cause difficulty.

preparing for completion

About a week before completion, you will have to inform the seller's solicitor of the amount of money you require at completion. Traditionally this is done by means of a completion statement, but where no apportionments are to be made and the amount consists of the price agreed, less any deposit paid by the buyer, it is easier and more usual to inform the seller's solicitor of the amount by letter.

outgoings

The rule is that the seller is responsible for outgoings up to and including the day of completion, and the buyer is responsible for outgoings thereafter. Outgoings include ground rent, general rate, water rate and sewerage charge. These last three items used to be apportioned by the seller's solicitor on completion. Nowadays, the apportionment is usually left to the relevant authority. If the seller has paid the outgoing in advance he gets a refund; otherwise he is billed for the period up to and including the date of completion. The buyer cannot be made responsible for arrears of general rate, water rate, or sewerage charge unpaid by the seller.

The Law Society's general conditions of sale endorse this practice of leaving the apportionment of rates etc to the relevant authority. There is an Oyez form, Conveyancing 46A, for this, on which to give to the relevant authority details of the property, the seller (and when he will leave the property), the buyer (and when he will acquire the property and become responsible for future payments), and ask for an apportionment. They will handle the matter from there on. The National conditions, on the other hand, do allow for the more traditional method of apportioning rates, etc, between the parties in the completion statement.

You can write to the various rating and water authorities informing them of your sale and the completion date, and ask them to give you an apportioned figure up to and including the day of completion. If by chance you have not paid the rates etc in advance, the buyer's solicitor may require you to give them an undertaking (on completion) to pay these up to completion. Strictly speaking, they have no right to ask this since the buyer cannot be made responsible for payment. But you should be willing to give such an undertaking; it can be in the form of a simple letter addressed to the buyer's solicitors promising to pay the relevant outgoings and stating the amount.

If your sale is governed by the National conditions and you decide to apportion the rates etc which you have paid up to a date later than the agreed completion date, then you will have to work out how much of the payment made is for the period between the day after completion and the last day covered by the payment, and show it on a completion statement. The buyer is responsible for this amount: it should therefore be added to the amount he has to pay on completion. If rates etc are in arrears (this is unlikely), do exactly the opposite. You will have to produce receipts on completion for any payments in advance you are claiming back from the buyer. Receipts are not given for general and water rate and sewerage charge unless specially requested. If you know you will be selling you should ask for receipts just in case you need them. Alternatively, you can get a letter from the local and water authorities confirming the date to which rates and charges are paid, and the amounts.

In the case of leasehold property, you will need a formal completion statement: ground rent and insurance premiums will have to be apportioned. Ground rent for a leasehold house is generally paid in arrears. As a result, the apportionment of ground rent is usually in favour of the buyer and something has to be subtracted from the money needed to complete, to cover the proportion of ground rent for the period for which no ground rent has yet been paid. Insurance is usually paid in advance. You will have to produce a receipt for the last premium on completion since you are requiring the buyer to pay a proportion of this.

If the buyer has, exceptionally, been allowed into possession before completion, the completion statement, besides perhaps apportioning the outgoings as from the date on which the buyer was allowed in (under the National contract only) will include an item for the interest on the balance of the purchase price. It is worked out on a daily basis: so-many three hundred and sixty-fifths of one year's interest at the appropriate rate per cent on the price less deposit.

Here is a specimen completion statement based on the assumption that rates are to be apportioned:

Stilton to Chalmers
9 Glen Drive, Minford, Surrey
Completion statement made up to 1 March 1986

	£	£
Purchase price		40,000.00
Less deposit		4,000.00
		36,000.00
Add		
Proportion of general rate from 1 March to 31 March 1986 (31 days) at £472.00 p.a.	40.09	
Proportion of water rate for same period at £49.00 p.a.	4.16	
Proportion of sewerage charge for same period at £51.00 p.a.	4.33	48.58
Balance payable on completion		36,951.42

the amounts of money

You should tell the buyer's solicitor exactly how you require the completion money to be paid, either on the completion statement (if any) or by letter. If you have an existing mortgage, you should have found out how much money will be needed to pay off the mortgage on the day fixed for completion (and to whom the banker's draft for the amount should be made payable). With this information you can work out how the completion money must be split: so-much to the building society or other lender, the remainder to yourself.

It might be more complicated than that. For instance if you are completing the purchase of another house on the same day as you are completing the sale of your present one, you would want to use whatever is left after paying off the old mortgage towards paying for the house you are buying. Your seller's solicitors may have asked you to provide the purchase money in two separate amounts. Furthermore, you may be having a fresh mortgage on the house you are buying and the amount to be advanced must be taken into account too.

The buyer's money is probably coming from at least two sources, too. If he is having a mortgage, and you are paying one off, you may expect that the completion moneys will in fact be split at least three ways and three banker's drafts will be produced at completion. (Keep calm and work it all out step by step. This is what happened at the completion of Matthew Seaton's purchase of 14 Twintree Avenue.)

Remember that if your sale is governed by the Law Society's general conditions of sale, the banker's draft for the completion moneys must be drawn on a CHAPS bank; under the National conditions a 'designated bank' (unless of course the special conditions specify another bank).

where to complete

You must also agree a a venue for completion. You can, by inserting a special condition, choose anywhere in England or Wales. So, in theory, you could ask that everybody should come to complete at your house, or the pub around the corner – but don't: a 'clever' d-i-y seller would only annoy the other side and may even lose the sale. If a mortgage is to be paid off, completion usually takes place at the seller's building society's (or other lender's) solicitor's office. The building society may, in fact, insist that completion takes place at the office of its solicitor because it will not release any of the deeds until its loan has been paid off (and the seller may find that he is charged a small fee for the solicitor's time involved).

If you have no existing mortgage to pay off, the buyer's solicitor's office will be the most likely place.

You should ask for completion to take place earlier than 2.30 p.m. (it must, under the Law Society general conditions; under the National conditions only if completion day is a friday) so that banking arrangements can be made on the same day.

Where seller and buyer live some distance apart, completion is often carried out by post. However, your buyer's solicitor probably will not agree to complete through the post with a seller acting on his own behalf. If you have an existing mortgage, your mortgagee's solicitor could be asked to act as your agent for a postal completion. Otherwise, the buyer's solicitor will probably instruct another solicitor in your town to act as his agent for completion.

before completion

You should execute the transfer, to have it ready for completion. This involves signing the transfer in the space indicated (alongside the 'seal' which is a little red sticker) in the presence of a witness, who should countersign the transfer and add his or her name, address and occupation. Any co-seller should also execute the transfer in the same way. The transfer should be left undated until completion.

The seller does not need to make any complicated preparations for completion. You will usually only have to take along the transfer. If you have no mortgage, you will have to provide the land certificate (and the lease, in the case of a leasehold house). You may also have to produce evidence of payment of outgoings for the buyer's solicitor to inspect, and of course, hand over the keys or tell the estate agents that they should do so after completion.

The buyer (or someone on his behalf) may well ask if he can inspect the property before, or on, the morning of the completion day. You should make the arrangements for him to do this. It is an important part of his pre-completion arrangements.

completion

The procedure followed at completion will be similar to that followed at the completion of Matthew Seaton's purchase of 14 Twintree Avenue (see pages 145 to 148).

The solicitors of your mortgagee will probably begin the proceedings by handing the charge certificate to you. Make sure that it is the right one and hand it to the buyer's solicitor. The same procedure usually applies to form 53 or an undertaking to provide it. If you have no existing mortgage to pay off, hand over the land certificate instead.

Next comes the transfer. This will be undated and you should confirm that the buyer's solicitor wishes that the transfer should bear the date on which completion is taking place. When you have dated the transfer, hand it to the buyer's solicitor. He will then pass it to his client's mortgagee's solicitor with the mortgage deed and any other items required. At this stage you might also be required to show the buyer's solicitor receipts or other evidence that any relevant outgoings have been paid and/or hand over an undertaking to pay any outstanding bills for them.

getting the money

Now the money is paid over. The buyer's solicitor will produce banker's drafts totalling the amount required to complete, as notified by you. Check that they are made out as requested. If you are discharging a mortgage, hand over to your lender's solicitor the draft that is made payable to him or to your lender.

Finally, the deposit has to be made over to you. If it was paid to an estate agent, you will require a deposit release from the buyer's solicitor addressed to the estate agent. Send the deposit release to the estate agent immediately after completion and request him to send you a cheque for the amount of the deposit. If he acted as agent for you on the sale of your house, you will find that he deducts his commission from the amount of the deposit.

If the deposit has been held in a joint account at a bank in the name of, say, the buyer's solicitor and yourself, the buyer's solicitor should hand you a cheque signed by him drawn on that joint account. You then countersign the cheque and present it in the normal way, and the account is closed.

The buyer is entitled to go into occupation of the house immediately the sale is completed. You should therefore now hand the keys to the buyer's solicitor. If it is more convenient, leave them wth the estate agent and hand the buyer's solicitor the letter addressed to the estate agents authorising them to hand the keys to the buyer.

If by any chance completion is delayed, the procedure described on pages 148/149 is applicable to both sales and purchases.

afterwards

After completion, do not forget to cancel the insurance (except in the case of a leasehold house, where the insurance is generally taken over by the buyer). Strictly speaking you could have cancelled the insurance as soon as contracts were exchanged, as the house was the buyer's responsibility from then on. But it is best to maintain the insurance until the money is in your hands. A seller who has a mortgage may, by the terms of his mortgage, have to keep the property insured until the mortgage is redeemed, at completion.

And remember to have the electricity and gas meters read on the day you move out, to notify British Telecom, to make arrangements with the post office regarding the forwarding of mail. You should, of course, cancel the instructions to your bank if you have been paying off your previous mortgage by banker's order. These, however, are practical matters: the legal side of selling the house is over.

SPEEDING THINGS UP

The outline conveyancing procedure on pages 194 to 196 shows fairly realistically, if somewhat optimistically, the time it takes to buy or sell a house with registered title absolute. The preliminary stage may be prolonged if, for example, the local authority is slow in returning the buyer's local search and enquiries, or if the buyer has difficulty in obtaining a satisfactory mortgage offer. Completion is not usually later than four weeks from the date of exchange of contracts, unless the parties have agreed to a later completion date.

At the beginning of 1984, a committee was set up by the government to look into the simplification of conveyancing "so that the public can benefit from a quicker and cheaper system". The committee reported to the Lord Chancellor in January 1985 and as part of their package for reducing the length of a domestic conveyancing transaction to three weeks, they made the following recommendations of relevance.

how to reduce stage 1 to two weeks

(a) The *seller* should make a local search and enquiries of the local authority immediately he decides to sell his property and send the replies together with his replies to standard enquiries before contract, to the buyer with the draft contract. This would save approximately two weeks and would necessitate a change in the present forms.

The objections to sellers' searches and enquiries are that they quickly become out of date and that a seller's idea of appropriate enquiries may not be the same as a buyer's.

(b) The buyer should obtain in advance of his 'house-hunting' an offer of a mortgage loan based essentially on his own personal creditworthiness, subject to the valuation of the particular property (to be carried out after contracts are exchanged) and to the availability of funds. This would mean building societies altering their current practice and expose the buyer to a greater risk than he faces at present, of not being able to finance his contractual obligation to buy. It would however save upwards of two weeks. One building society is now introducing a 'mortgage certificate' which confirms the applicant's status as potential borrower and the amount of loan available.

(c) There should be one form of contract for sale, prescribed by statute. This would involve a change in the law. At present the seller (or his solicitor) can use whatever form of contract for sale he likes provided it complies with certain basic formal requirements. He can invent his own or use one of the two standard forms of contract available on the market. One set form of contract would save time, especially for practitioners who would need to familiarise themselves with only one form instead of two.

how to reduce stage 2 to one week

(a) Lenders should confirm their mortgage offers on an oral valuation and should have standardised mortgage deeds.

This would involve building societies in a change of practice. At the moment they wait for their surveyors' written valuation reports and they each have their own individual (and slightly differing) forms of mortgage deed.

(b) Completion monies should be transferred via CHAPS, the system for the electronic transfer of funds. It is claimed to be fast, safe and efficient. Only certain banks are members of CHAPS and practitioners have to have access to a terminal to use it. Not all practitioners have such access. It is extremely unlikely that ordinary members of the public would be allowed to use the system in the foreseeable future.

None of these recommendations has as yet been universally adopted.

GLOSSARY

advance – the mortgage loan

authority to inspect the register – the document, addressed to the Land Registry, by which the registered proprietor (that is, the owner), allows someone else, usually the buyer or the buyer's solicitor, to be given information about the register of a property, usually to enable him to make an official search

bridging loan – a loan, usually from a bank, to tide a person over between the time when he has to pay the purchase price of one house and the time when the proceeds of sale of another and/or mortgage funds become available to him

charge – any right or interest, subject to which freehold or leasehold property may be held, especially a mortgage; also used to denote a debit, or a claim for payment

charge certificate – the certificate issued by the Land Registry to the mortgagee of a property which has a registered title, showing what is entered on the register of the property at the Land Registry (when there is no mortgage, a land certificate is issued instead to the registered proprietor)

charges register – one of the three parts (the others are the property register and the proprietorship register) which go to make up the register at the Land Registry of a property with a registered title. The charges register contains details of restrictive covenants, mortgages and other interests, subject to which the registered proprietor owns the property

completion – the culmination of the procedure in the transfer of a house, when the necessary documents are handed over in exchange for the purchase money

completion statement – an account prepared by the seller (or his solicitor), setting out exactly how much money should be paid by the buyer at completion, taking into account the price, the deposit and any apportionments

compulsory registration of title – the requirement in certain parts of England and Wales that any property, when next bought, should be registered at the Land Registry

conditions of sale – the detailed standard terms which govern the rights and duties of the buyer and the seller of a house, as laid down in the contract which they sign; these may be the National or the Law Society's conditions of sale

contract – any legally binding agreement; on the sale of a house this is the document, in two identical parts, one signed by the buyer and the other by the seller, which, when the parts are exchanged, commits both the buyer and the seller to complete the transaction by transferring ownership in exchange for paying the purchase money

conveyancing – the legal and administrative process involved in transferring the ownership of land or any buildings on it, from one owner to another

covenant – a promise in a deed to undertake (if covenant is positive) or to abstain from doing (if restrictive covenant) specified things

deed – a legal document which, instead of being merely signed, is 'signed, sealed and delivered'; the legal title to freehold and leasehold property can only be transferred by a deed

delivery – the handing over of a deed, after having been signed and sealed, with the intention that it should now be operative

deposit – part of the purchase price, usually ten per cent, which the buyer has to pay at the time of exchange of contracts. It can be forfeited to the seller if the buyer withdraws (through no fault on the part of the seller) after signing a binding contract

discharge of registered charge – a document by which a building society, or other mortgagee, acknowledges that all the money secured by a mortgage on a registered property has been paid; usually made on the printed form 53

early redemption – paying off a loan before the end of the mortgage term

endowment mortgage – a loan on which only the interest is paid throughout the term and which is paid off at the end with the proceeds of an endowment insurance policy

engrossment – the actual deed or document which is executed or signed, as opposed to a mere draft of it

enquiries before contract – a set of detailed questions about many aspects of a property which the seller, or his solicitor, is generally asked to answer before the buyer is prepared to sign a contract; also called preliminary enquiries

enquiries of local authority – a number of questions asked of a local authority on a printed form about a particular property; the form is usually sent with, and loosely speaking forms part of, the buyer's local search which is made before contracts are exchanged

exchange of contracts – the stage at which the buyer has signed an engrossment of the contract and sent it to the seller, and the seller has done the same in return, so that both become legally bound to go through with the transaction (many solicitors 'exchange' over the telephone, but not with a do-it-yourself conveyancer)

execute – to sign and seal a document

fee simple – freehold

filed plan – the Land Registry plan by reference to which a particular registered property is identified in the property register

fixtures – articles, such as boilers, baths and tv aerials, which, because they are attached (by screws, concrete or pipes, for instance) to the house itself, as opposed to standing supported by their own weight, are presumed to have become legally part of the house itself, so that they are included in a sale, unless specifically excluded by the contract

form 53 – the form on which a mortgagee acknowledges that a mortgage of a property with a registered title has been paid off; the discharge of a registered charge

freehold – the absolute ownership of property, as opposed to leasehold

good leasehold title – the description given by the Land Registry to the title or ownership of a leasehold property having a registered title, where the Registry is entirely satisfied about the owner's entitlement to the lease itself, but has not enquired into the ownership of the freehold or other superior title of that property

ground rent – the rent paid to the landlord by a leaseholder who owns a leasehold property.

joint tenants – two (or more) people who hold property as co-owners; when one dies, the whole property automatically passes to the survivor(s) (this is in contrast with what happens in the case of tenants-in-common)

land certificate – the certificate issued to the registered proprietor of a property which has a registered title, showing what is entered on the register of that property at the Land Registry. When the property is mortgaged, no land certificate is issued (it is retained at the Land Registry) and instead a charge certificate is issued to the mortgagee

Land Charges Registry – a government department in Plymouth where rights over and interests in unregistered land are recorded. Charges are registered against the name of the owner, not the land concerned. The register is open to public search. (Not to be confused with the Land Registry, which deals only with properties where the title is registered)

Land Registry – a government department (head office in London and district registries in various other places in England and Wales) responsible for opening, maintaining and amending the registers of all properties in England and Wales which have registered titles. Not to be confused with the Land Charges Registry, which deals with properties which have unregistered titles.

Law Society – the solicitors' professional body

Law Society's conditions of sale – one of the available sets of standard terms incorporated into a contract for the sale of a house and so governing the rights of the buyer and the seller; another such set is the National conditions of sale

leasehold – ownership of property for a fixed number of years granted by a lease which sets out the obligations of the lease-holder, for example regarding payment of rent to the landlord, repairs and insurance; as opposed to freehold property, where ownership is absolute

legal charge – a mortgage, especially one framed so as to include the words 'legal charge'

lessee – the person to whom a lease was originally granted, and, more commonly, the present leaseholder

lessor – the person who originally granted a lease; also, the present landlord

local authority – district council/county council/borough council responsible for roads, planning, social services and many other local matters on which rates are spent

local land charges register – a register kept by the local authority, containing charges of a public nature affecting the property, which is consulted by the local search

local search – an application made on a duplicate form to the local authority for a certificate providing certain information about a property in the area. Also denotes the search certificate itself. A local search should reveal whether the property is likely to be affected by compulsory purchase, whether there are any out-standing sanitary notices, and similar matters. Loosely speaking, a local search also includes the answers given by the local authority to a number of standard enquiries, made on another special form; these answers are usually obtained at the time when the local search is made, but technically they are not part of it

mortgage – loan (usually for house purchase) for which a house is the security. It gives to the lender (usually a building society or bank) certain rights in the property, including the power to sell if the mortgage payments are not made. These rights are cancelled when the money advanced is repaid with interest, in accordance with the agreed terms

mortgage deed – the document enshrining the mortgage conditions

mortgagee – one who lends money on mortgage, such as a building society, bank, local authority, insurance company or private lender

mortgagor – one who borrows money on mortgage, usually to enable him to buy a house

National conditions of sale – one of the available sets of standard terms incorporated into a contract for the sale of a house and so governing the rights of the buyer and the seller of a property; another set is the Law Society's conditions of sale

office copy – an authenticated copy of an official document issued by the department or organisation which holds the original

official search – an application to an official authority (such as a local authority, the Land Registry or the Land Charges Registry), to find out some relevant facts about a particular property

overriding interests – rights which are enforceable against a property, even though they are not referred to on the register of the property at the Land Registry; for instance, the right of a weekly tenant to remain in possession after the house has been sold, even though no mention of his tenancy is found on the register

possessory title – the description given by the Land Registry to the title or ownership of a property where, due to some defect in the title, the registry is not entirely satisfied as to the owner's ownership of the property, but only satisfied that he is lawfully in possession of the property

preliminary enquiries – enquiries before contract

property register – one of the three parts (the other two being the proprietorship register and the charges register) of the register of a property with a registered title, setting out an exact decription of the property concerned

proprietorship register – one of the three parts (the other two being the property register and the charges register) of the register of a property with a registered title, setting out the name and address of the registered proprietor – that is, the present owner

real property – land, in particular freehold land, and any buildings on it

register – in the case of a property with a registered title, the record for that property kept at the Land Registry, divided into the property, the proprietorship and the charges registers

registered proprietor – the person who is the owner of a property which has a registered title and is shown as such in the proprietorship register at the Land Registry

registered title – title or ownership of freehold or leasehold property which has been registered at the Land Registry, with the result that ownership is guaranteed fully or to some degree by the state; in many parts of the country, registration of title is compulsory

repayment mortgage – loan on which part of the capital as well as interest is paid back by regular instalments throughout the term of the loan

requisitions on title – questions asked in writing by or on behalf of a buyer or mortgagee about matters concerning the seller's ownership of the property, and about other matters arising after exchange of contracts, as opposed to enquiries before contract

restrictive covenants – obligations imposed by covenants on the owner of a freehold property, preventing him from doing certain things on his property, such as opening a business or putting buildings on certain parts of it

road charges – the charges imposed on the owners of properties along a road for the cost of making up or repairing the road, usually according to the frontage of each property

sale by private treaty – the most usual method of selling a house or flat when property is put on the market, a buyer found, the terms of the sale agreed between seller and buyer, surveys and searches made, while the whole matter is 'subject to contract'; as against selling at auction where there is exchange of contracts the moment the house is knocked down to the buyer

scale fee – a fee calculated by reference to the price being paid, or money being borrowed, rather than to the amount of work involved, for example an estate agent's fee

seal – a small red disc stuck alongside the signature on a deed

search – an enquiry for, or an inspection of, information recorded by some official body, such as a local authority, the Land Registry or the Land Charges Registry

search certificate – the certificate of the result of a search

solicitor's undertaking – a letter signed by a solicitor in which he personally guarantees something; it is his professional duty to honour such an undertaking, even though he may suffer financially as a result if his client defaults

stakeholder – one who holds a deposit as an intermediary between buyer and seller, so that the deposit may only be passed on to the seller with the permission of the buyer, or returned to the buyer with the permission of the seller

stamp duty – a tax payable to the government on some deeds and documents, including deeds of transfer, conveyance or assignment of property at a price above (at present) £30,000; deeds and documents cannot be used as evidence or registered at the Land Registry unless they are properly stamped

subject to contract – provisionally agreed, but not so as to constitute a binding legal contract: either the buyer or the seller may still back out without giving any reason

tenant for life – a beneficiary who is entitled to receive the rent or other income from, and/or live in, property during his lifetime only, after which it will pass to others, in accordance with an existing will or trust

tenants-in-common – two (or more) people who together hold property in such a way that, when one dies, his share does not pass automatically to the survivor but forms part of his own property and passes under his will or intestacy (this is in contrast with what happens in the case of joint tenants)

'time is of the essence' – if a party is late in performing a contractual obligation where time is of the essence, the party not in default is released from his corresponding contractual obligation. For example, if a buyer fails to make his requisitions on title on time, the seller does not have to answer them. Completion time can be made of the essence in a contract for the sale of land by either party serving a 'notice to complete'

title – ownership of a property

title absolute – the description given by the Land Registry to the title or ownership of a freehold (and sometimes leasehold) property where the registry is entirely satisfied about the owner's ownership of the property; being registered with title absolute means that ownership is guaranteed by the state

title deeds – deeds and other documents which prove ownership of freehold or leasehold property. They normally consist of each deed transferring ownership over the previous fifteen years or more, together with mortgage deeds. Where the title is registered a land certificate takes the place of the title deeds or, if there is a mortgage, a charge certificate issued by the Land Registry

transfer – a deed which transfers the ownership of a freehold or leasehold property, the title to which is registered at the Land Registry (as opposed to the deed used where the title is unregistered, which is a conveyance in the case of a freehold, and an assignment in the case of a leasehold)

trustee – a person in whom the legal ownership of property is vested, but who holds it for the benefit of someone else (called a beneficiary)

trustees for sale – people who hold property as trustees on condition that they should sell the property, but usually with a power to postpone doing so indefinitely if they want to

vendor – the seller

OUTLINE CONVEYANCING PROCEDURE

(when a buyer is found immediately and there are no delays anywhere)

STAGE I – PRELIMINARY

WEEK	SELLER	BUYER
	Decides to sell	Looks for and finds house
	Obtains copy entries on register and filed plan from district land registry (*form A44*)	Finds out about mortgage
1	Agrees to sell Prepares draft contract and sends it to buyer with copy of entries on register and filed plan →	Agrees to buy
		Receives the draft contract and other documents
		Applies for mortgage, instructs surveyor
2		Makes local land charges search (*form LLC1*) and enquiries of district council or London borough (*form Con.29A or D*)
	←	Sends enquiries before contract to seller (*form Conveyancing 29 Long*)
	Replies to enquiries before contract →	
		Considers seller's replies to enquiries before contract
		Receives from local authority: replies to local land charges search and replies to enquiries building society or bank: mortgage offer surveyor: reports on state of property
3		Makes: personal inspections of the property and at local authority (re planning etc)
	Agrees contract	Agrees contract
		Arranges insurance of property
	Signs contract, exchanges with buyer's, receives buyer's deposit ⇄	Signs contract, exchanges it with seller's, and pays deposit

STAGE II – CONTRACT TO COMPLETION

WEEK	SELLER	BUYER
		Studies copy of entries on register and filed plan
	Sends to buyer authority to inspect the register (*form 201*) →	
		Prepares requisitions on title (*form Con.28B* and draft transfer (*form 19 or 19JP*)
5	←	Sends requisitions on title and draft transfer to seller
	Replies to requisitions on title and returns draft transfer to buyer →	
		Considers replies to requisitions on title
		Sends to solicitor of building society (or other mortgagee): results of local search enquiries before contract and enquiries of the local authority with replies contract copy of entries on register and filed plan authority to inspect the register requisitions on title with replies approved draft transfer
7	Notifies own mortgagee about redemption and obtains redemption figure and 'daily rate' in the event of delay	Receives draft mortgage deed and mortgagee's requisitions on title
	←	Raises further requisitions with seller if necessary
	Replies to further requisitions →	
		Returns requisitions to mortgagee with replies
		Requests mortgagee to specify the amount that will be provided on completion
	Prepares and sends completion statement →	
		Makes official search of register (*form 94A and form 201*)
		Makes 'bankruptcy only' land charges search (*form K16*) if required by mortgagee
8	←	Engrosses transfer and sends to seller
	Informs rating authority of date of sale and requests apportionment of rates etc (*form 46A*)	Fills in forms for Inland Revenue [(*form Stamps L(A)451*) and Land Registry (*formA4*)
	Arranges for handing over keys	Obtains banker's draft for own part of completion money
		Inspects property

STAGE III – COMPLETION

	SELLER	BUYER
same day	Produces land certificate or charge certificate and transfer Produces receipts for outgoings Dates transfer Hands over: land certificate or charge certificate form 53 or undertaking for discharge of mortgage transfer keys or authority for keys	Checks copy of entries on register and filed plan against land certificate or charge certificate Looks at receipts for outgoings Pays all the completion money (from self and mortgagee) Dates mortgage deed

STAGE IV – AFTER COMPLETION

	SELLER	BUYER
	Redeems own mortgage Forwards form 53	If no mortgage: gets transfer stamped and lodges application to be registered as new registered proprietor (*form A4*) at district land registry (if mortgage, mortgagee attends to stamping of transfer and registration of dealings) If buying leasehold property, registers transfer with landlord (or notifies as appropriate) Applies to district land registry for copy of entries on register and filed plan (*form A44*)

INDEX

INDEX

The front and back pages of the National Conditions of Sale, Twentieth Edition, on page 160 of this book are reproduced by kind permission of Oyez Stationery Ltd; and those of The Law Society's Contract for Sale (1984 Revision) on page 161 by kind permission of The Law Society.

HOME AND DRY

the video cassette for do-it-yourself conveyancers

This entertaining and down-to-earth 30-minute video follows the steps of a fictional Emma and Matthew Seaton as they go about buying their first home. It has been shown on television (Channel 4) as the first video cassette to accompany a CA book.

The HOME AND DRY video cassette is available on VHS or Betamax. On its own, it costs £19.95 (together with this book £24.95).

Which? way to buy, sell and move house
takes you through all the stages of moving to another home – considering the pros and cons of different places, house hunting, viewing, having a survey, making an offer, getting a mortgage, completing the purchase, selling the present home. It explains the legal procedures and the likely costs. Buying and selling at an auction and in Scotland are specifically dealt with. The practical arrangements for the move and for any repairs or improvements to the new house are described. Advice is given for easing the tasks of sorting, packing and moving possessions, people and pets, with a removal firm or by doing it yourself, and for making the day of the move go smoothly.

living with stress
helps the reader to identify the sources of stress in his own life – following a bereavement, in a job or in unemployment, in marriage or before or after divorce, in loneliness or in overcrowding. It lists the common warning signs and indicates what steps to take in order to adapt successfully or change what needs to be changed.

earning money at home
for anyone who wants or needs to take up an activity at home that will bring some extra (or essential) cash, this book sets out what is entailed. It puts forward the pros and cons of working at home, stressing the self-discipline required and the reorganisation that may be necessary. The statutory requirements about planning permission, liability for insurance, national insurance and tax are all explained. Advertising and getting work, costing and charging for it, getting supplies, keeping accounts, are all important factors that are fully covered. The second section of the book suggests some types of work that might be suitable, with or without previous experience, giving a brief account of what may be involved in undertaking them. Courses for brushing up a skill or hobby to a more professional standard are suggested, and sources of further help and advice are given. The final section discusses what to do if your venture fares badly and, more optimistically, how to expand the business when successful.

starting your own business
is a competent guide to the best way of making a success of a new venture. It leads the way from the first essential step – defining exactly what product or skill you have to offer – to warnings of pitfalls and difficulties. It deals with sources of capital, how to raise it, legal requirements, pricing the product, marketing and selling, premises, keeping accounts and other records, VAT and other taxes, staff relations, insurance, thinking about computers. Sources of advice and information for the small businessman are given throughout the book.

divorce – legal procedures and financial facts
explains the financial facts to be faced when a marriage ends in divorce. It includes getting legal advice, legal aid and its drawbacks, the various orders the court can make. Fictitious case histories illustrate different personal situations and alternative solutions.

householder's action guide
deals with problems and decisions a householder may have to face, and what actions he should take to assert his rights and fulfil his obligations. It explains the rights and duties of the local authority towards the householder, and yours to them; it deals with rates and how to appeal against an assessment. Other topics include legal liability towards visitors, tresspassers and casual passers-by; determining the exact location of boundaries, recognising structural and maintenance faults, employing a builder, obtaining planning permission, how to deal with nuisance caused by other people's children, their animals, noise in the street or from the flat next-door, how to avoid disputes with neighbours and, if it is unavoidable, what action to take.

wills and probate
stresses the advisability of making a will, explains how to prepare one, sign it and have it witnessed. It also explains what would happen on an intestacy (that is, dying without a will) and warns that a person's property may reach unforeseen beneficiaries (including the crown). It gives examples of different types of wills showing consideration for the effects of capital transfer tax. The section about probate deals in detail with the administration of an estate without the help of a solicitor, the valuation of the estate, payment of tax, the steps involved in obtaining probate, the distribution of the estate in accordance with the will, the transfer of property to the new owner, explaining clearly the procedures involved at every stage, and the various problems that might arise.

what will my pension be?
sets out in its three main sections what you can expect to get from the state pension, your employer's pension scheme or (if you are self employed) retirement annuities. Throughout, the tax implications are clarified, and hints given on how to improve your future pension.

what to do when someone dies
explains factually and in detail all that may need to be done: from getting a doctor's certificate, reporting a death to the coroner where necessary, registering the death, getting the various death certificates. Differences between burial and cremation procedure are discussed, and the arrangements that have to be made, mainly through the underetaker, for the funeral. The book details the various national insurance benefits that may be claimed.

children, parents and the law
explains the legal rights and duties of a parent to a child (and vice versa), how much say a parent has regarding a child's religion, education, medical treatment, marriage at various ages. It deals with the effects of illegitimacy; the legal aspects of adoption; children being looked after by a non-parent: guardianship, custodianship, fostering, children in the care of the local authority or a ward of court. Other chapters include children and the criminal law, contracts with children, injury to a child and legal aspects of a parent's death.

taking your own case to court or tribunal
is for people who do not have a solicitor to represent them in a county court or magistrates' court or before a tribunal. This book tells you the procedures to follow in preparing and presenting your case, what happens at the hearing, what steps can be taken to enforce a judgment, how to appeal if the judgment goes against you. It explains in layman's terms how to conduct proceedings yourself in the county court (arbitration for 'small claims' and open court hearings), in the High Court (rarely appropriate for a litigant-in-person), in a magistrates' court (for both civil and criminal matters), at a social security appeal tribunal (challenging a DHSS benefits decision), before an industrial tribunal (dismissal cases).

Consumer Publications are available from Consumers Association, Castlemead, Gascoyne Way, Hertford SG14 1LH and from booksellers.